BAMBOO
ITS CULT AND CULTURE

BAMBOO
ITS CULT AND CULTURE

PAINTINGS
BY
WANG TSENG-TSU
IMPERIAL PRINCE PAINTER

INTERPRETATIVE TEXT AND ART ANALYSIS
BY
KATHERINE M. BALL

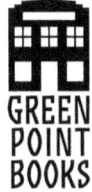

GREEN
POINT
BOOKS

For information, address:
Greenpoint Books
767 South 4th Street
Philadelphia, PA 19147
info@greenpointbooks.com

Paper: 979-8-88677-000-1
Cloth: 979-8-88677-002-5

Cover design by
Michael Schrauzer

TO THE

GLORY

OF

GOD

For God is not unrighteous
To forget a labor of love.

Hebrews 6:10

PREFACE

The motive for writing this book, entitled "BAMBOO, ITS CULT AND CULTURE", is to bring to art-minded people a reproduction of a part of an album of Chinese paintings of great merit and distinction.

It includes reproductions of but ten of the album's collection, which were chosen for their adherence to the code of "Universal Art Principles." However, notwithstanding they are reproductions, they reflect the charm and beauty of the originals.

To promote a better understanding of this book the following description of the album is given. It is fifteen inches square and bound within unpainted wooden covers. The pages, following the Chinese tradition, open back and forth, accordion-fashion, the first page occurring where the occidental reader looks for the last. The text is arranged in vertical columns, to be read, successively, from right to left, and from top to bottom. On its opening wooden cover, there is pasted a white paper label, inscribed with the following five Chinese characters written in black ink:

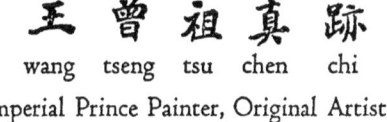

王　曾　祖　真　跡

wang　tseng　tsu　chen　chi

Imperial Prince Painter, Original Artist

It contains fifty-five paintings of Bamboo and a double page of calligraphy, consisting of a memorial to the painter by his friend and tutor, Lu-chi Yung.

The paintings are done in what is known in the Flowery Kingdom as *mo-tsu*, "Bamboo in black ink." Each has an inscription and seal, but no signature of the painter—for it would have been regarded as an act of bad taste for a painter of rank and power to reveal his identity.

The inscriptions are done in the running grass hand, consequently readable, but the seals are not only of ancient pattern, but badly drawn and cut, hence undecipherable.

The paintings convey, psychologically, the noble qualities of the plant, particularly as revealed under the varying conditions of wind and weather. They are distinctly legible, and, in drawing, follow nature's organic forms, strictly adhering to laws of growth.

While the work of this painter is that of an eighteenth century technician, it still represents an art which had its inception in the Golden Period of the early T'ang dynasty days. And, although this painter was unfamed because unheralded, he has proved that he not only had the vision and understanding of a genius—as well as an exceptional training—but a profound enthusiasm for the ancient "Cult of the Bamboo," a cult which was responsible for one of the greatest moral and spiritual uplifts of mankind—an uplift which ultimately led to what was then known as the ideal "Superior Man."

And, although this cult had its origin in so humble a source as a plant, it exalted the Chinese nation to a first rank among peoples—a fact to which contemporaneous Chinese refer with great pride. According to the inscriptions of the paintings, the work was begun about 1701 and completed in 1703, while the memorial, written by Lu-chi Yung, is dated 1706.

It has not been feasible to make an absolute reproduction of the original album, but there has been a serious endeavor to apply in this semi-occidental book the spirit of such important fundamentals of Chinese art as Simplicity, Restraint and Elegance.

I am quite aware that I am blazing a new trail, and expect to share the fate of the pioneer. All I ask is that I be judged by righteous judgment. I foresee much variance of opinion and welcome it, particularly when given by scholars of art erudition, for then I feel sure it will be constructive and of the kind that will promote my own growth.

I apologize for the omission of the names of some of the occidental translators of the quoted Chinese poems, names for which I diligently searched, but was unable to find. And I feel quite penitent for having had the audacity of "falling into verse," knowing that writing poetry is regarded as almost a crime in my own country.

(8)

The production of this book has not been entirely an unalloyed task. Research in many fields, and contact with authors and collectors, has liberally compensated me for all expenditure of effort and energy, while the formation of the code of "Universal Art Principles" has been a most interesting achievement. For my ability to accomplish this, I acknowledge my indebtedness to a great teacher, Miss Caroline E. Powers of the Cooper Union Art School of New York City.

I was young, still in my teens, but susceptible to being inspired. And now, in my advanced years, I recall her saying with impressive emphasis: "You must be a growing entity; a perpetual student. You must live your art, both privately and professionally, and you must be an art missionary;" to all of which, I have striven to be steadfast.

This code of "Universal Art Principles," to which I have referred above, has proved to be of great value to me, particularly in defining the significance of the Canons of Hsieh Ho.

To others to whom I am indebted, I desire to make additional acknowledgment for generous and helpful service.

To Dr. Ray Lyman Wilbur, Chancellor of Stanford University, not only for the beautiful tribute he has paid to me in the Foreword he has written for my book, but for his sympathy and encouragement during this period of professional problems.

To Professor Guy Gayler Clark, dean of the Cooper Union Art School, for his Foreword, in which he expresses his appreciation of my humble efforts in writing and book-making.

To Professor Cheng Chi-yu of the University of California not only for his Foreword but for his contribution of calligraphy by which the pages of my book are so beautifully decorated.

To Ying Kiang-Kang-hu, for translations and interpretations extending over several years of my first struggles with the inscriptions of the original paintings.

To Dolores Cadelle of the San Francisco Public Library, for her exceptional devotion in connection with much necessary research.

To George M. Pring, for an unwavering devotion and self-sacrifice over years—without which this book would not have been written.

To Grace Ahlers and Muriel Fournier for many acts of helpful service during this chaotic period of the "duration."

To Will D. Robertson and other members of the Gillick Press staff, for their patience and devotion in carrying out my own ideas of book-making applicable not only to Chinese Art, but to the art of all countries.

I am sincerely grateful,

Katherine M. Ball

CONTENTS

CANON VI—Pertains to the perpetuity of ancient ideals. Studying masterpieces of all times, and transmitting the principles governing them as to subject matter, as well as to technique.

History testifying to psychology being the determining factor in the esthetic worth of art. Psychology, benefic and malific.

The psychology of geometric units, ranging through lines, straight and curved; planes and solids, and objects classified under these heads.

The psychology of surface characteristics of objects, such as color and texture; and of motion; and of patterns of beauty in nature—including effects of steam, fog, clouds, rain and snow.

Psychology the source of human behavior—the classification and definition of the five fixed stations of activity determined by the individual's evolutionary status.

Pictures defined as the Literary Man's Painting. Absence of color, not regarded as a lack, since black is felt to include all color.

Illustrations—reproductions, yet reflecting the artistry of the originals. No attempt to define any species of Bamboo, but to stress generalities of characteristics.

Modes and moods of joyousness or despondency, expressed under varying conditions of wind and weather, attributed to the activity of a dominating psyche.

Principles of *Yang* and *Yin* definitely expressed in the "pattern" and "no-pattern" or "space of silence," of the design.

The subtle quality of pure esthetics, manifest in that nameless something which is rather felt, than seen, commonly acclaimed as charm—a quality akin to "it," when referring to the attractiveness of a great personality.

But above and beyond all, the quality that impels the art student's desire to acquire more knowledge of the science of the subject, a knowledge that may urge him on to a life of Righteousness, as defined in the ancient poem entitled "The Royal Road of Righteousness."

INTRODUCTION

In my preface I have spoken of my motive for writing this book. Here I desire to relate the circumstances which led to its undertaking.

It was not a case of seeking either fame or gain, but to respond to an inner urge, to release a strong conviction.

My first book, "Decorative Motives of Oriental Art," was quite a different matter. That was forced upon me by circumstances. I was obedient to a demand, and conscientiously devoted to it, ten years of my entire leisure, sacrificing every personal indulgence in order to accomplish it.

Here again I have similarly given years of my leisure to bring to a fruition my endeavor. These years were necessarily somewhat interrupted by other interests, but the work of the book continued consistently over the period from 1929 to the present time.

During the intervening years I had the marvelous experience of an odyssey through the Orient. This had increased my fund of knowledge and greatly extended my horizon. Therefore, on the resumption of my writing—after my return to this country—I found that what had already been done, did not conform to my later views and had to be redone.

And now after many frustrations, I am happy in the realization of its completion.

The experience which actuated this work is a matter of history which I feel may interest my readers.

I had been reveling in the beauty of a collection of ink paintings contained in a Chinese album. The dealer saw my interest and said to me: "Why do you not buy it?" I smiled and retorted: "I have just seen the price mark, and am not quite equal to five hundred dollars."

Then one day I met him on the street. He stopped and said: "I am in need of money. Would you consider the purchase of my book if I gave it to you at a bargain? Could you pay a hundred and fifty dollars?" As he said this I had a strange experience. It seemed as if a voice spoke to me, saying: "You are always boasting of being an art missionary. Here is your great opportunity! Buy the album, select from the fifty-five paintings the ten most attractive. Have them reproduced, write a brochure on Chinese painting, particularly applied to Bamboo. Make it a book especially designed for a living-room table, where both the members of the family and guests may be exposed to it. Make it so beautiful that it may do your missionary work."

At once the decision was made. I said: "Send it to me this evening."

And now, "BAMBOO, ITS CULT AND CULTURE" has reached its maturity and I cannot refrain from quoting: "The desire accomplished is sweet to the soul."

The inception of this book began with the thought of Art, but its consummation concludes with the theme of Righteousness—Righteousness, the channel for the rejuvenation and regeneration of mankind.

May
BAMBOO, ITS CULT AND CULTURE
ever bless
the household where it lingers.

FOREWORD

Katherine M. Ball has had a lifetime association with art and giving instruction to young and old. Had she not become interested in art she would have been a scientist. Her approach to art and to life in general is on a factual basis. She believes in art and in its wide acceptance as one of the significant ways to regenerate the human race and to give it new incentives and inspiration. Beauty with her is not a cult but a way of living in closer and more affectionate harmony with our environment. With beauty life can be attractive and good for all. All that is needed is what Pasteur called "the prepared mind" so that one can understand excellence. Then rich or poor, young or old, no one can be cheated out of some of the best things open to human beings. Sunsets can be seen free; beautiful trees border most horizons; and light and shade are everywhere.

Miss Ball's book, with its central theme of bamboo, carries us back into the contemplative and philosophical life of the wise and patient Chinese. We can all profit by the methods she describes by which we can learn to understand and to value beauty. What she gives us is the way to prepare our minds so that there will be an enhancement of those lovely and pleasurable sensations that give charm to all forms of beauty.

FOREWORD

Although during the past two or three generations artists have been deriving fresh inspiration from the Orient in small doses, it has remained for Miss Ball to become a leader in our extensional orientation and to find out at first hand what the Far East is all about. She has been delving deeper than most and has arrived at the heart of the fire where others had been halted by the smoke. Her work in this field is helping us to overthrow many of the academic formulas and esthetic traditions which for so many centuries have been based almost exclusively upon "the glory that was Greece and the grandeur that was Rome."

The value of her message is greatly enhanced by Miss Ball's scholarly assignment of easily comprehended categories to the trends and significances of oriental Art. Her approach and interpretation are somewhat unique in that they blend text and picture in a single idiom. Motif and motive are to her as inseparable and herein lies her distinct contribution bearing the rich fruit of conscientious research and intuitive comprehension.

This work serves as an illuminating sequel to the exhaustive survey presented by her "Decorative Motifs of Oriental Art" which so satisfied our occidental curiosity some years back in regard to the poetic parables and precepts hidden behind our oldest surviving culture. There is more than meets the eye in these good books, though what meets the eye alone would still deserve our grateful admiration. It should accordingly exert an influence inspiring the student to worthier effort in the design and content of his own creating. He should not mistake the rule for the principle nor be tempted to indulge in slavish imitations of a foreign mannerism but should see and heed in these masterpieces that still, small voice of beauty and truth whose message is universal. Kipling was wrong when he said of East and West that never the twain shall meet.

Guy Gayler Clark

FOREWORD

I esteem it a great honor to be asked to write a Foreword for Miss Ball's book "Bamboo, Its Cult and Culture".

Finding that the book contains all the necessary subject matter, as well as the exemplification of the technique of the painting, I shall aim to concentrate my efforts upon the practical value of the book, as well as on the ability and achievement of the author.

Miss Ball's esthetic insight and knowledge derived from a profound experience of many years of the study of art in its universal sense, enabled her to discover an example, which ultimately became the source of the material for this book.

I am happy to say I have seen these paintings, and find that they portray, not only spiritual qualities and behavior of bamboo, but the special technique practiced in the Golden Age of China, when it was the custom to paint bamboo with black ink, or what was then known as *mo-tsu*.

This exceptional book also reveals to its readers, the symbolism of the philosophy, which regulated the particular life of the Chinese scholars of this historic period—so beautifully told in Miss Ball's poem, "Bamboo Symbolic".

Again, the ten collotypes which supply the principal illustrations of the book, not only reproduce the qualities of their originals but constitute its main charm.

During the eight years of war, China has sustained a loss of many of her valuable art treasures. Other materials which are thus lost are replaceable but not great art. Therefore, Miss Ball is to be commended for her intelligence and foresight in collecting and preserving this material, not only for the Chinese world of culture of this era, but for all posterity. She, therefore, has the hope

(19)

that through the medium of her book, she may contribute an element toward bringing about a better relationship between oriental and occidental peoples.

Cheng Chi yu

BAMBOO PICTURESQUE

Bamboo! How fraught with grace, refinement and charm, is the sound of this word.

Bamboo! Clustering in groves; green stalks upright, feathery plumes of tender hue
reaching toward the sky.

Bamboo! Roseate at dawn, golden at sunset, grey at dusk; and then—the luster
of the leaves at night, silvered by the moon.

Bamboo! Dimmed by a veil of fog, concealed and revealed in turn by driving sheets of rain; swayed
by gentle breezes; wildly tossed by the winds; yielding to the weight of the snow.

Bamboo! In calm erect; but bent in storm—ever beautiful.

BAMBOO SYMBOLIC

Constancy, for its never changing color, remaining ever-green during
all seasons of the year.

Rectitude, for its resilience before the merciless typhoon, ever bending
but never breaking, however old and dry.

Fidelity, for its patient resignation while bearing the weight of the winter snows.

Integrity, for its honesty in ever splitting straight and even, when cut.

Purity, for its virtuous heart, which is ever clean and white.

TRANSLATION OF THE MEMORIAL

A Dedication of the Work of the Painter of Bamboo, Wang Tseng-tsu—Imperial Prince Painter by Lu-chi Yung, his tutor and friend.

I am only a poor scholar unaccustomed to writing a dedication. The Prince, however, notwithstanding the difference in our social stations, had most graciously favored me not only with his friendship, but with his affection. I therefore feel it a privilege to undertake this obligation.

The Prince was a man of great dignity yet never haughty and of great nobility of character. He was famed in the empire for his generosity and beloved for his kindly and generous treatment of every associate. He gave liberally of his time to the service of the State, while spending his leisure in his library in quest of Truth.

He was especially noted for his painting of *mo-tsu*, "bamboo in black ink." For five years I had the opportunity of seeing him at work and observed that, unlike an ordinary painter who is obliged to labor for results, he drew not only with great ease, directness, spontaneity and power, but in a style both individual and elegant.

Su Shih, better known as Su Tung-p'o, the famed poet and art critic of the Sung dynasty, once said, "Nothing can compare with the art of painting; among all pleasure-giving things it is the most enjoyable;" and in describing a painting by Wen Hu-hou, he said, "Whether the bamboo consists of the small gnarled and twisted kind that creeps along the ground, or of the variety that is as large as a sword blade ten feet long, the painter should have a clear and definite idea of its important features and characteristics before he takes up his brush."

Such was the feeling and the habit of the Prince. Furthermore, had he not refrained from the self-indulgence of eating meat and rich foods which stupefy the mind; from the association of women and degrading music which dwarf the soul. And had he not discerned the subtle qualities of the art of the ancients and followed their precepts, he could never have portrayed so much beauty.

(25)

Realizing his greatness, I feel myself most incompetent and unworthy to even attempt to enliven the spirit of his paintings. Since, in spite of my insignificance, he treated me as a national character and on his deathbed honored me by requesting that I write interpretive inscriptions on all his works, I shall, in all humility, strive to gratify his wish.

But as I turn the leaves of this album, I grieve! For all is changed—the Prince is gone—the Pine is laid low—the Tree has fallen—I feel my tears flowing and close the book and think. I can see his form and features. I can hear his voice.

Again I look at his work and I know that he is not dead for his spirit dwells within it. Just as the light of a precious gem ascends heavenward illuminating all space, so do these beautiful paintings emit a radiance which words fail to describe. The ideas they convey will live on undefiled from generation to generation. Their portrayal cannot be misrepresented by reproduction, burned by fire, or otherwise destroyed by any element.

Such is the *mo-tsu* of my Prince!

Therefore washing my hands and submissively bowing, I take up my brush and write my commentary at the end of this album.

Shan Yin District. K'ang Hsi era (*circa* 1706 A.D.), 44th year, 7th month, 15th day, three days after the full moon.

Lu-chi Yung, official designation, Tzu En, personal name.

THE CALLIGRAPHY OF THE MEMORIAL
BY LI-CHE YUNG

婁起榮手書紀念王曾祖文

我生平手跡以今葉為之誌自惟固陋不足傳　王之萬一願念

數年來方將布衣幅巾從　王於蘇湘涵素間而日月傾易松

崩木壞有捲苓欷歔不知深之何從者然微末如榮而　王且以

國士目之身後而此兩傳之手澤命榮為傳之則固榮之感激知己

蓋見　王之道德深遠土壤細流而在必納而傳神小技能使一片

靈臺羅作虔楮彷彿我

王之音容左而神理未嘗歇絕心吾聞玩琰珙璧異寶所聚必有光氣愵作

層霄而傳之世之石不可以洫火不可以燹其我

王斯墨竹之謂與謹盥手再拜秉筆而跋其後

時康熙四十四年歲五乙酉秋七月中元後

三日山陰姜起榮弁書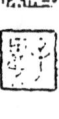

榮窮巷顓生無文章伎能傾動名公鉅卿謬蒙我 王

王尊賢禮士屈王公之貴而折節寒素固令憶之閱五年於兹矣心 王

下交於榮之切也榮浮知 王之深 王貴不自伐高不自矜鴻

功雅量已照人耳目惟於蒲骰

皇獻之暇圖書墳典莪不玩其奥而探其微而於丹青墨竹一家尤能事妙

天下云宋蘇軾謂物之可喜且以悦人者莫若畫而其記文湖州

畫貲嘗谷偃竹也曰自蜩腹蚭蚹以至劍拔十尋者必先浮筭

竹於胸中而後振筆直追其見 王之於此藝也游墨揮毫娛

戲焉己爾而瀟灑曠遠自成一家獨出筆畦墨吟之外若與夫

怊怜專壹之士較其毫釐分寸者非夫屏膏梁遠色聲研精

霧騰春日永示浩瀚

LIFTING FOG, FRESH SPRING DAY

Revealing Endless Immensity

霧騰春日示浩瀚

籊籊竹竿以釣于淇
豈不爾思遠莫致之

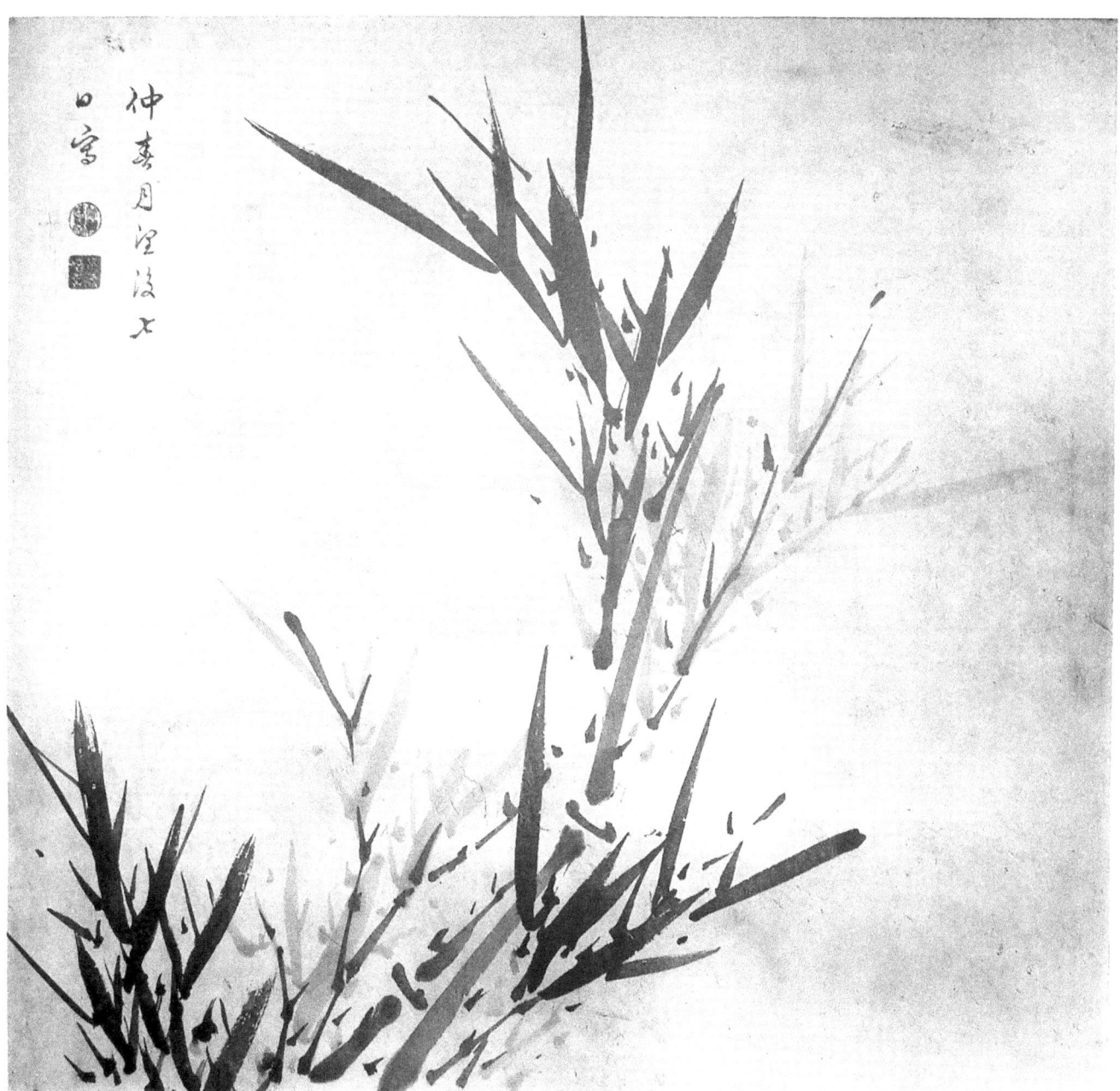

雨後落葉靜中自在

DRIPPING LEAVES AFTER THE RAIN

Self-realization in quietude

雨後落葉靜中自在

鏘兮鏘兮風其漂女
叔兮伯兮倡予要女

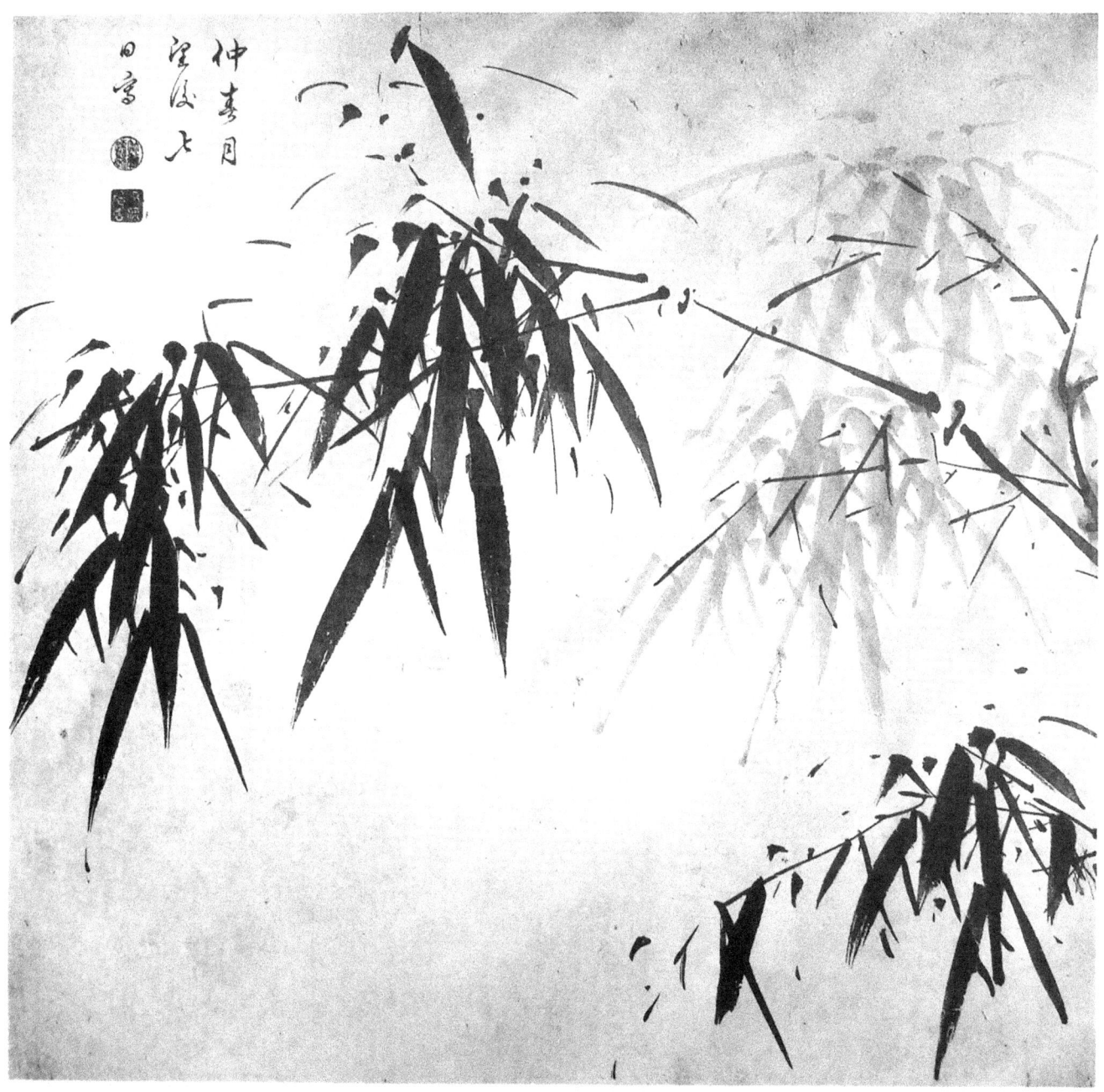

夜月輝耀沈著高矜

GLISTENING UNDER THE FULL-MOON'S
RAYS OF A QUIET NIGHT
Elated yet placid

夜月輝耀沈著高矜

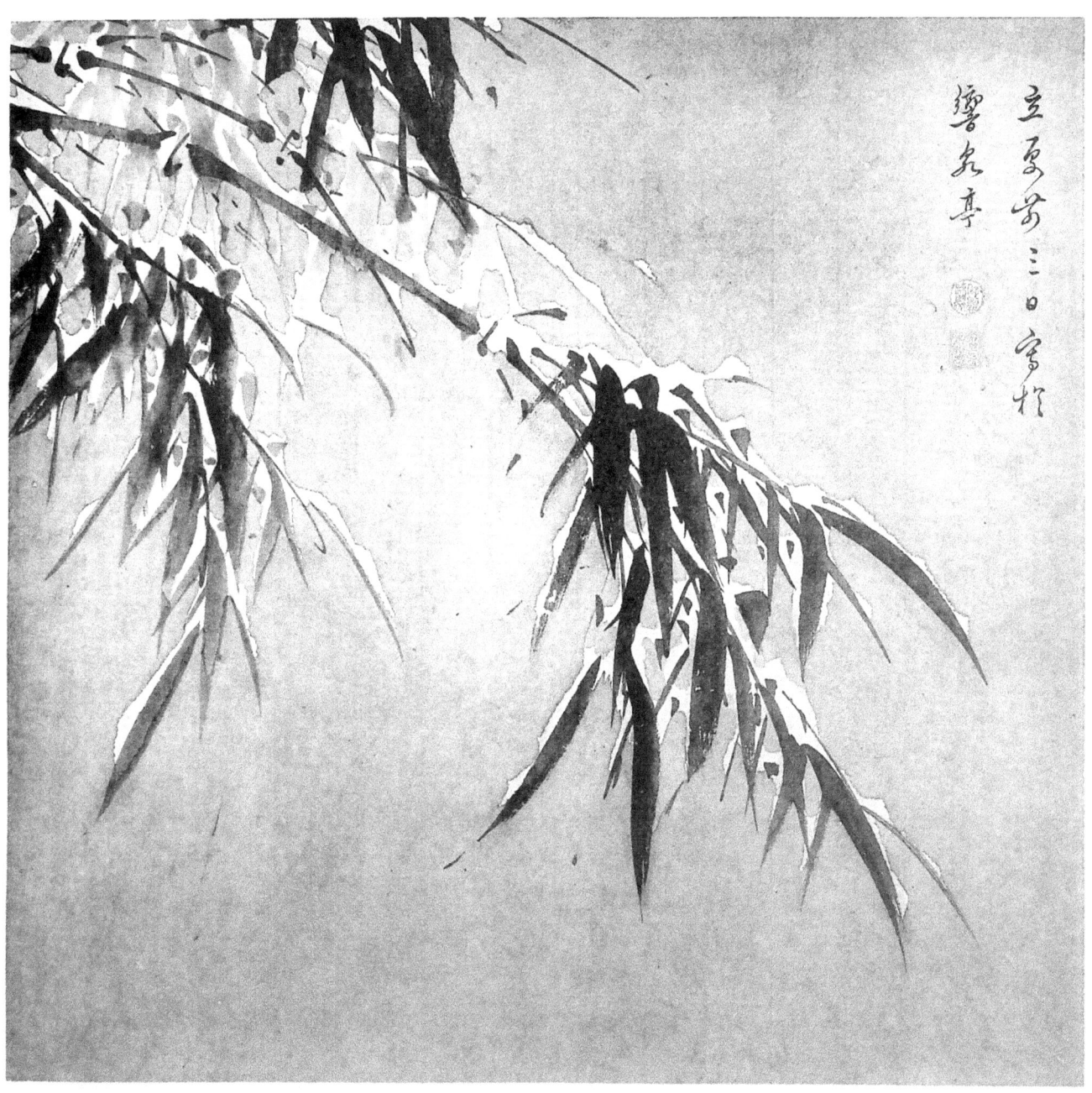

霧晨風嚴物本洪荒

VIOLENTLY TOSSED BY THE WIND ON
A FOGGY NIGHT

All things created come out of chaos

霧晨風緊物本洪荒

秩秩斯干幽幽南山如竹苞矣如松
茂矣兄及弟矣式相好矣無相猶矣

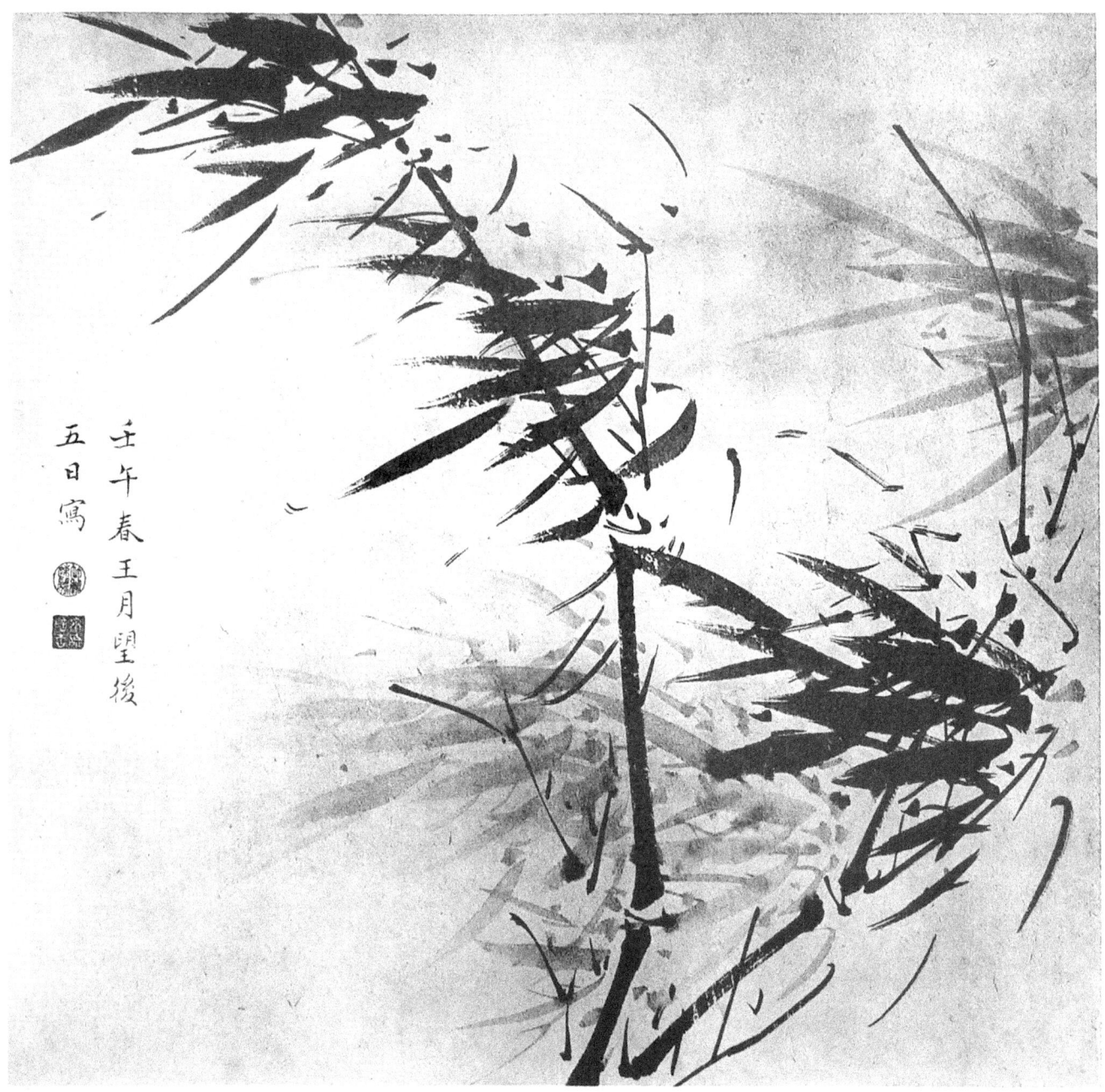

颶後恬寧虛寂太空

TRANQUILITY AT EASE AFTER THE STORM

Naught but deep silence reigned o'er a void

颱後恬寧虛寂太空

瞻彼淇奧綠竹猗猗

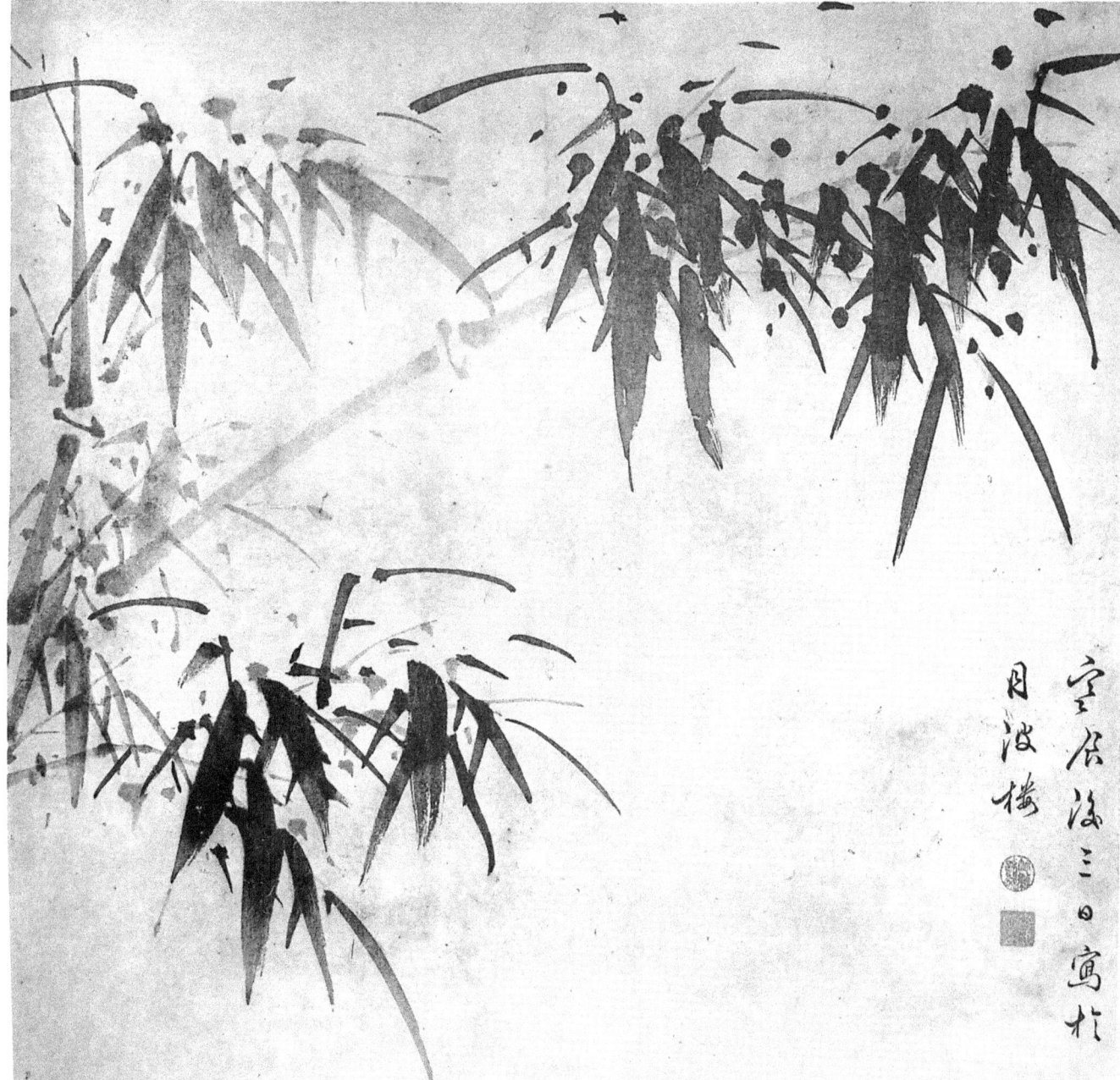

空居海三日寫於
月波樓

春月戴雪怡然起興

SNOW-LADEN, BRILLIANT IN THE SPRING
FULL MOON

Exhilaration with tranquility

春月戴雪怡然起興

松竹可以耐雪霜
明智可以涉危險

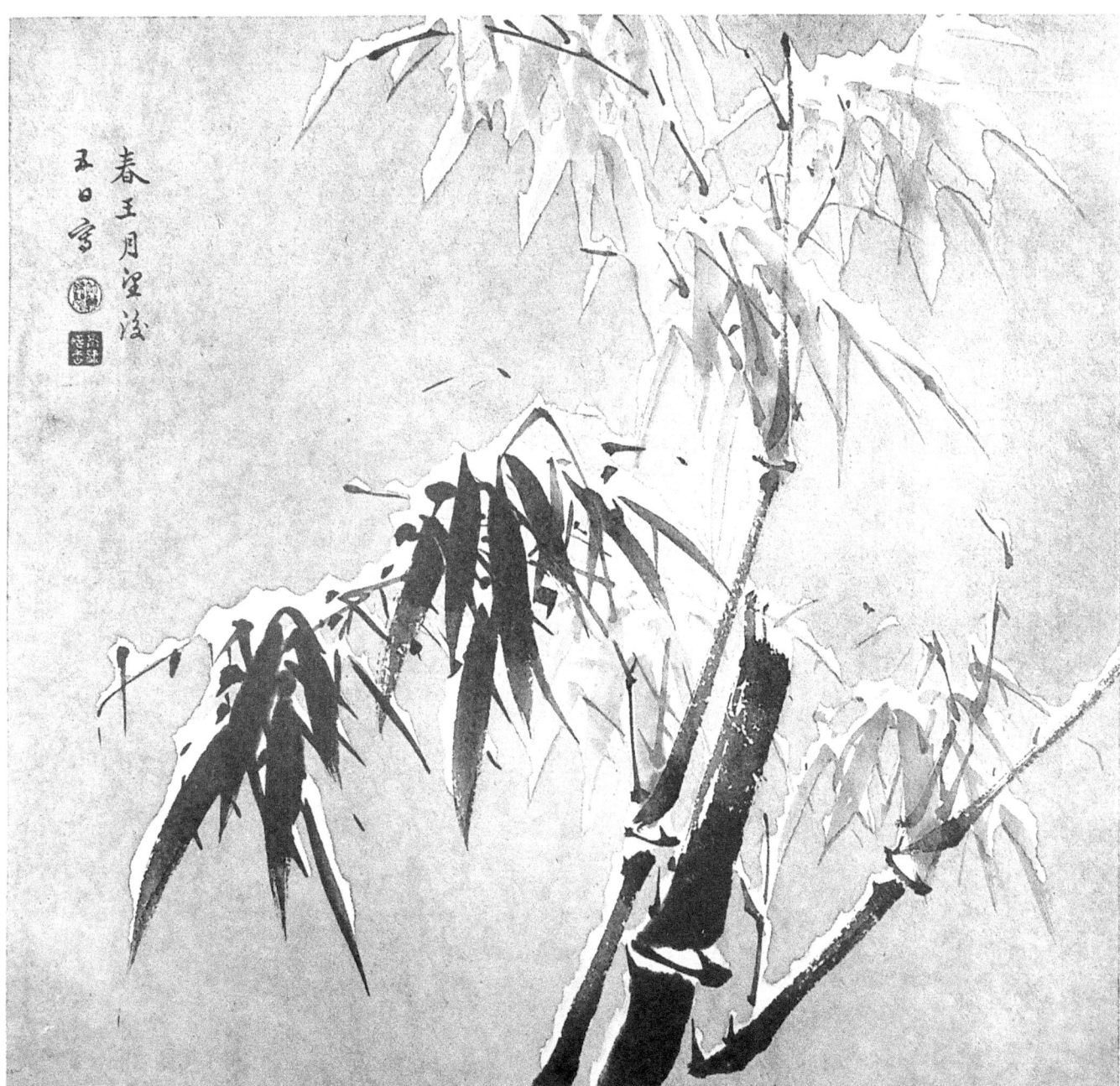

晨露助趣織默愉忻

ENLIVENED BY THE DEW OF DAWN, IN A
LOWERING MIST

Exultant in the stillness

晨露助趣織黙愉忻

松竹梅歳寒三友

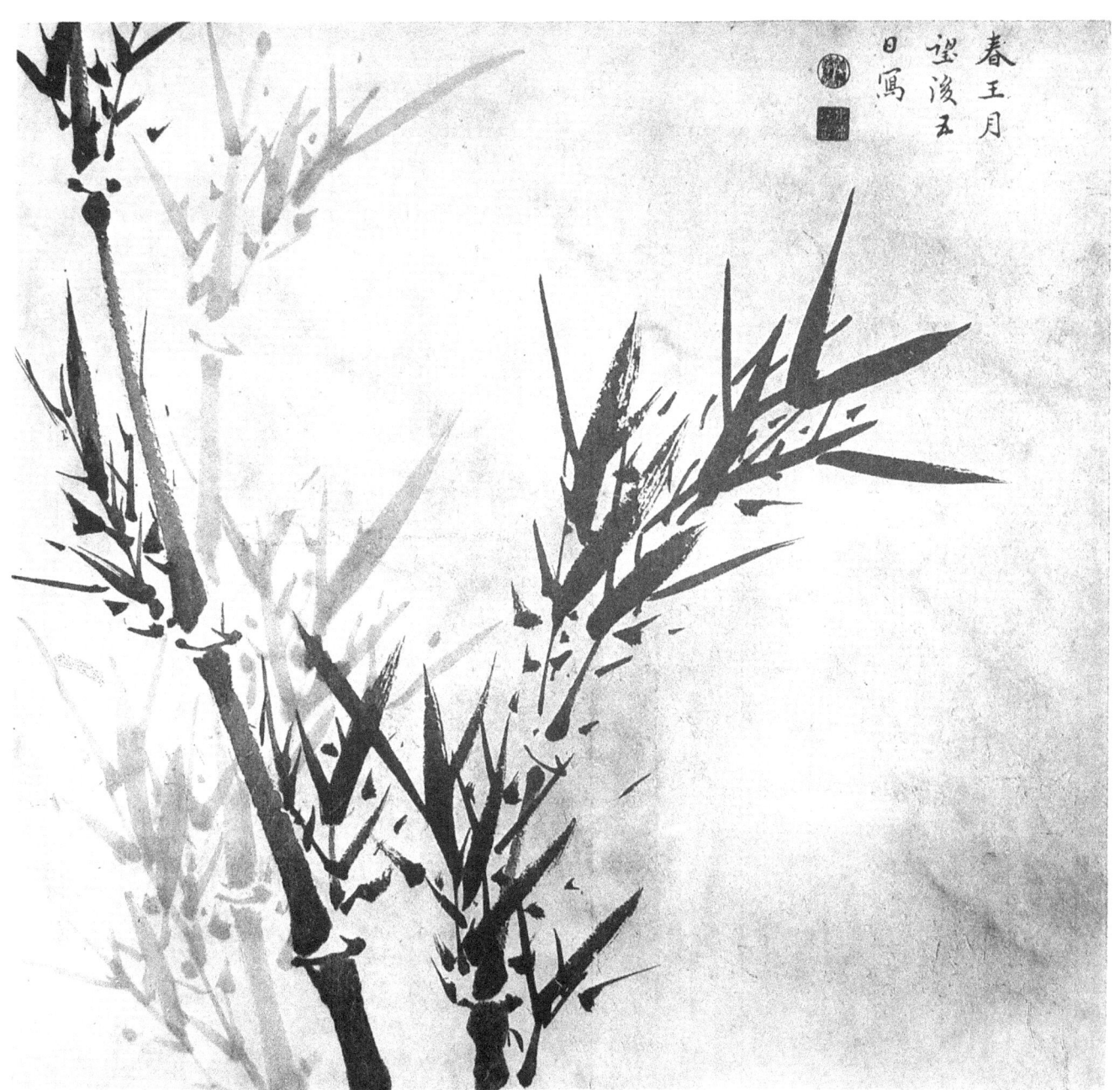

飄搖震撼兩慇風儴

TOSSED BY THE WIND OF AN APPROACHING STORM

Tumult and Distraction

飄搖震撼雨憊風僝

無肉令人瘦無竹令人俗

寧可食無肉不可居無竹

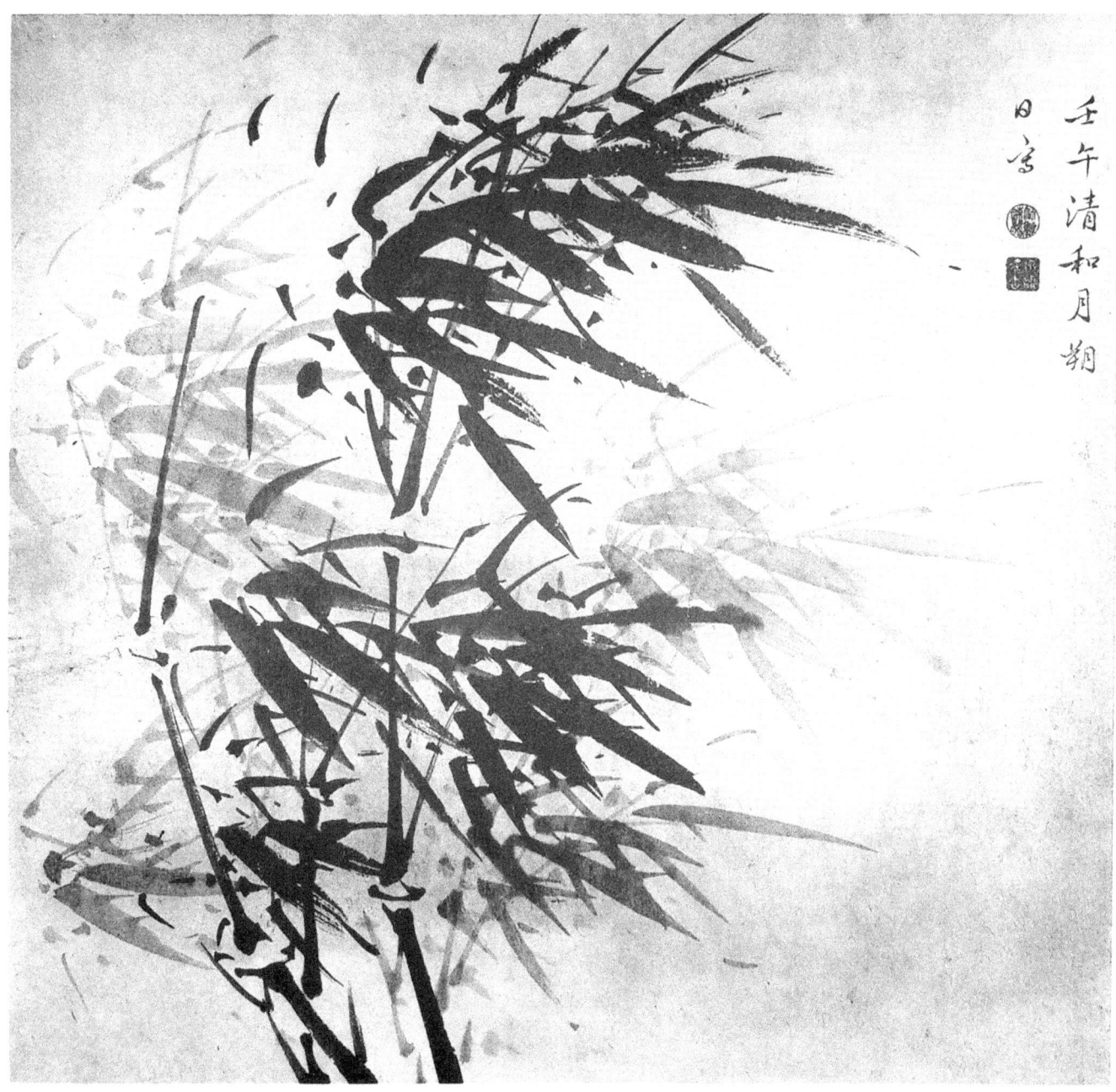

壬午清和月朔
日寄

白日積雪讓遜墾忍

BEARING THE WEIGHT OF SNOW ON A GRAY DAY

Submission and endurance

白日積雪謙遜堅忍

竹本無心清且雅
蘭雖是草秀而香

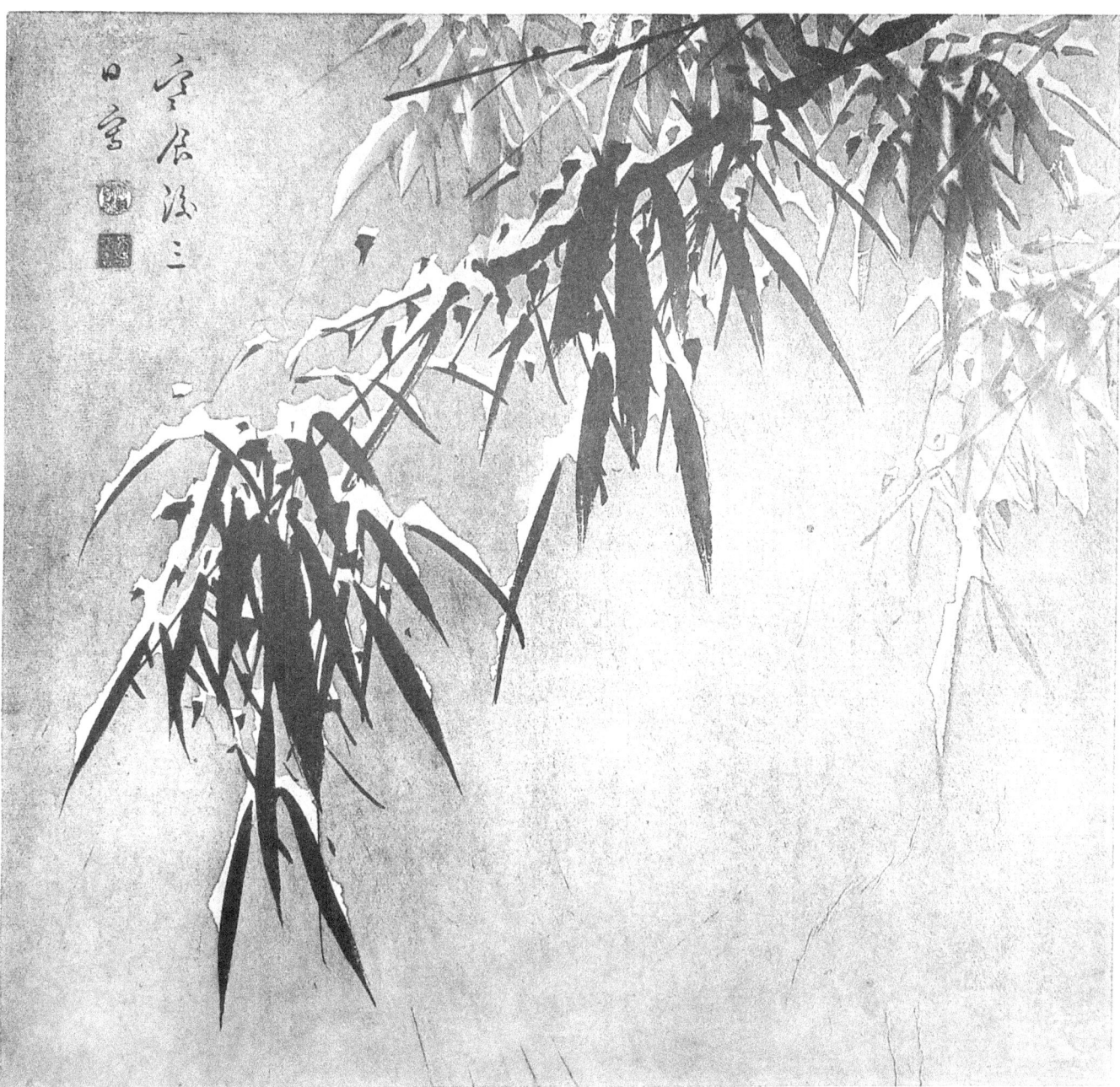

拂曉風吹靜而不息

WIND-BLOWN AT DAWN
Unsettled yet calm

拂曉風吹靜而不息

下莞上簟乃安斯寢乃寢乃興乃占

我夢吉夢維何維熊維羆維虺維蛇

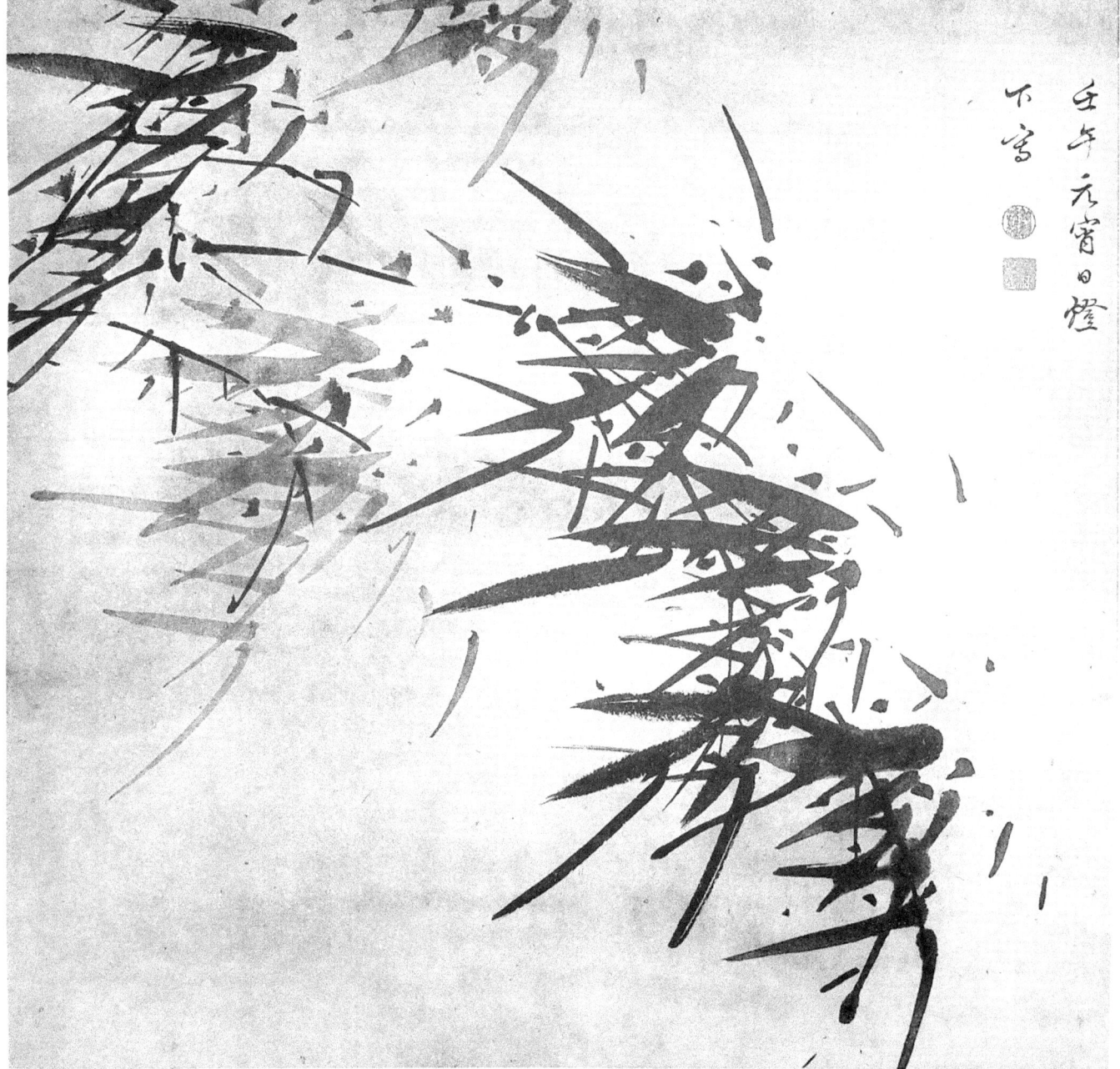

BAMBOO IN USAGE AND ART

From the very beginning of Chinese history, this giant grass has been a subject of almost sacred significance. So intimately has it been associated with the life of the Oriental peoples, that its very name conjures up a vision of the Far East. The purposes which Bamboo have rendered to the Eastern world through the ages have been manifold, always serving, not only the physical, but the esthetic and spiritual needs of man.

The Western world, both through imports and travel, is quite familiar with its many uses. The practical ones, from the larger function of supplying material for the construction of buildings —palace or hut—to the making of the simplest domestic utensils, and even to the furnishing of one of the most important foods. There is abundant proof that poets were moved to expression by its practical, and also esthetic, aspects.

KUO FU writes:

> *Tao Chih, "plum blossom Bamboo" is useful*
> *as well as beautiful.*
> *It adorns the landscape;*
> *Offers shade on a warm day;*
> *Supplies materials for mats*
> *So that we may sleep in comfort;*
> *And provides a staff of support for old age.*

And from *Po chu-i,* of the T'ang dynasty:

> My new province is a land of Bamboo Groves;
> Their shoots in spring fill the valleys and hills.
>
> . . .
>
> I put the shoots in a great earthen pot
> And heat them up along with the boiling rice.
>
> . . .
>
> Now every day I eat them recklessly;
>
> . . .
>
> All the time I was living at Lo~Yang
> They could not give me enough to suit my taste.
>
> Translator—Waley

And from *Tu Fu* of the Sung dynasty:

> The wind blown Bamboos,
>   Sweep my windows and darken my room,
> Though the hour be but noon.
>   Their tender green leaves
> Washed by the summer showers
>   Catch the soft breeze,
> Cool my wine, though the air be heated,
>   And refresh my hours of quiet
> With cool fragrance.
>   My trees are still young,
> But with care and time
>   They may yet pierce the floating clouds.

Similar evidence may be found in the following poem by *Tai Tung*:

In my garden grow many Bamboos
To comfort and cheer my hours of study.
In summer and winter alike
They are ever beautiful.
Their graceful plumes sweep my windows
Like the shadow of the dragon or
Droop over the quiet pool
Like the tail of the phoenix.

Still another usage of Bamboo is given by the poet *Su Tung p'o* of the Sung dynasty, who stressed the significance of the Bamboo Grove:

We may eat without meat
But we cannot live without Bamboo.
To be meatless, we will become weak;
To be Bambooless, we will become unclean
    and worldly.
If we are weak and thin
We may be cared for by medicine
    and become strong and plump;
But if we are unclean and worldly,
No medicine can cleanse us.
The only remedy is to roam through the
    Bamboo Grove.

These groves, of which there were many, were known as Chu Lin. They were popular retreats for scholars and philosophers, who retired there to discuss and solve weighty problems. The most famous, the King Liang, flourished in the third century. It is said to have covered about three hundred square miles and was the property of the Imperial Household. In addition to being the haunt of scholars, it was also the scene of many social festivities. Since then, all descendants of the Imperial Line have been said to come from the Bamboo Garden. These retreats have also been a popular theme with painters. One subject in particular, Chu Lin Che Hsieh, "The Seven Wise Men of the Bamboo Grove," may still be found in many Art Collections.

After considering the practical aspects of the usage of Bamboo, we come to the place it holds in the field of Art.

The earliest paintings of Bamboo were definitely calligraphic in character. Though always remaining abstract, they appear to tend toward the actual characterization of nature. However, while the process seems to be a gradual change or growth from the ideograph to the semblance of a likeness, it is never factual, but always abstract. The abstraction—ever adhering to the organism of nature—revealing in the simplest possible form the bare essentials of the plant.

Later calligraphy—of which the Chinese speak as "inking or writing"—is expanded into painting. Since both required the same brush and methods, it was customary to refer to writing thoughts, rather than painting them. Regarding this, *Chao Meng-fu* of the Yuan dynasty once wrote:

> *Painting and writing are fundamentally the same,*
> *To paint a rock is to write it in the Fei-pi style,*
> *To paint a tree is to write it in the Choa style,*
> *And, if you desire to write Bamboo successfully,*
> *You must be familiar with the various styles of*
> *the calligraphy of all times.*

All training for painting began with the studies of Bamboo since it was considered the simplest of all models. At the same time, it presented problems which students have found difficult to solve. And though painters of varying degrees of ability have aimed to express its rare spiritual qualities, very few have ever succeeded.

However, it is said of Prince Chun—son of the Emperor Ying Tsun of the Sung dynasty—that, "As a painter of Bamboo in black and white—while portraying its luxuriant foliage and jointed stalks bowing in the breeze, sparkling in the dew, sweeping the clouds, or sifting the moonlight—he captured every charm." His wife, also, was a painter and calligrapher. Due to her great ability in rendering the truth of nature, she was accused of copying shadows of the plant which had been cast on her walls. The same has been said of others who were able to produce exceptional effects, by copying the deep shadows cast on a white wall by a brilliant moon.

Another successful painter of Bamboo was Hsieh Yueh of the T'ang dynasty. His method was quite the reverse of the above, as he spent much time in producing a single picture, repeating and repeating, until he felt he had reached his goal. Upon one occasion he presented to the poet, Po Chu-i, of the T'ang dynasty, a drawing which inspired the following poem:

> Of all plants the Bamboo is the hardest to draw,
> In ancient and modern times, many have tried,
>   but none have succeeded.
> The brush of *Hsieh Yueh* alone has been effective.

History records a woman-painter of Bamboo, *Kuan F'u-jen* who not only excelled in this field, but originated a new style. She wrote a treatise entitled "The Bamboo in Monochrome," which is still regarded as an authority. The Boston Museum possesses an example of her work.

Another painter who distinguished himself in this line was *Cheng T'ang.* His favorite variety was the Phoenix-tail Bamboo, the stalks of which are very heavy and bend over in a curve, while the leaves appear to sprout in a backward direction.

He ascended the famous Mt. Omei in the Szechwan province to see another variety of the plant, the Bodhisat or P'u-sa Bamboo.

This unquestionably derived its name from the sacred phenomenon, which pilgrims throughout the centuries have made great sacrifices to see and worship, since it was believed to be a revelation of P'u-sa Hsien, the elephant-riding deity of the *Amitabha Triad*—who personifies the Buddhist qualities of love, compassion and mercy—and presiding deity of the mountain.

This deity is said to have revealed himself to the monk Po-yen, which experience as well as the immensity and grandeur of the mountain, led him to select the latter as a place for meditation in seeking his enlightenment.

The phenomenon—which is scientifically accounted for—is often referred to as "The Brocken Spectre," a name derived from the place where it was first seen, Brockenburg in the Hartz Mountains of Germany.

The Brocken is merely the upper part of the body of the observer, occupying the particular spot where it intercepts the sun's rays. The one occurring on Mt. Omei is said to be that of the abbot of the monastery in that locality, who is able by this means to inspire the veneration of the devotees. In times past the faithful have been so moved by it, that they cast themselves into the abyss below, imagining they would be caught up in the arms of the P'u-sa and be borne to Paradise. There were other manifestations of a mysterious nature, due to the phosphorescence, which quite commonly collects in damp and swampy places. These picturesque legends, evolved from an imaginative interpretation of natural phenomena, seem to be but another instance of the magical miracles in which Buddhism abounds.

Of the painter Cheng T'ang—referred to above as ascending Mt. Omei to paint his favorite Bamboo—it is related that he also visited Elephant Hill, located in the vicinity, and secured drawings of other varieties of Bamboo, including those known as the Purple Bamboo, the Bitter Bamboo, the Wind Bamboo, the Tortoise-marked Bamboo and the Filial-piety Bamboo.

Another painter of Bamboo was no less a personage than the Emperor Hui Tsung, 1101 A.D., famed for his portrayal of the falcon. On one of his pictures, entitled "Bamboo and Birds," the great *Chao Meng-fu* of the Yuan dynasty inscribed the words: "What joy for trivial things to be limned by a master-hand that is divine."

The above mentioned Emperor-painter, *Hui Tsung*, in the first year of his reign, established an Imperial Art Academy. Here the Chinese students were given a training not only in calligraphy and painting, but in poetry as well. The three arts were so closely related that they were practically regarded as one, each functioning as an expression of the same idea, particularly in the inter-relation of painting and poetry. Chinese teachers always held that "A picture is a voiceless poem, and a poem a vocal picture," implying that the actual poem and picture have a natural poetic and pictorial correspondence.

An illustration, which occurs in the following poem, not only ably reveals the picture, but adequately describes a subjective epigrammatic rendition of it:

With ten strokes he built a mountain,
With two strokes a tree —
And then with the most delightful smile
He gazed through the lattice door awhile,
And with one stroke brushed in the boundless sea!
Lillian Miller, Contemporary American Poet

Others, of both ancient and modern origin, are in similar vein.

Sitting alone where the Bamboo grows,
The harp sings to me its tune,
Hid by the trees where no man knows,
I am greeted by the light of the moon.
Wang Wei —T'ang Dynasty
Arthur Waley —Translator

However, the visualization of a poem or a picture by different individuals varies greatly. Legend tells of a competition, held by the aforesaid Emperor Hui Tsung at the Imperial Academy, in which the competitors were called upon to express in graphic form, the poem, "The Bamboo Enveloped the Inn by the Bridge." The inn was featured by all but one contestant, with little attention given to the Bamboo. The successful competitor, however, subordinated the inn, permitting it to be merely glimpsed through the luxuriant and graceful foliage.

The Chinese have ever held that the great painter or poet must possess the quality of inwardness, which enables him to efface himself. He does not go through life making his art the outlet for his personal feelings; but strives to induce in the observer, emotions of a noble character, since it is his purpose to unite in his work the spirit of human life with that of the life of nature.

CANONS

The chief purpose of Chinese painting has ever been to reveal the life and spirit of the things portrayed, and the art form by which these ideas were expressed has always been regulated by the most rigid rules.

As far back as the Ch'i dynasty, in the fifth century, the poet and critic, *H'sieh Ho*, formulated Six Canons of Painting. These have been accepted and recognized by most Chinese painters from that remote time to the present day, and may be said to be responsible, not only for many of the masterpieces of Chinese Art, but also for much that is open to criticism, when subjected to a tribunal of intellectual psychological analysts.

While the author of this book fully appreciates the worth of Chinese painting, and realizes she has derived her greatest inspiration for growth from its serious study, she likewise understands its limitations, when regarded from a universal outlook.

Chinese art, with all its greatness, is but the art of a single nation, yet at present the only one from which to move upward while going onward. The Canons of H'sieh Ho are most confusing, and, to the western mind, almost irrational. Yet they contain "the kernel of the nut" which deserves cracking.

All Occidental writers on Chinese painting speak of H'sieh Ho's Canons, implying much, while saying little. In the given interpretation of them, the writer aims to blaze a new trail by using them as happy rungs of a progressive ladder, and humbly offers her matter as the result of much research, combining her findings in a code, which she offers as *"Universal Principles of Art."*

H'sieh Ho's Canons are apt to be difficult for the student of the West to understand in many respects. Quite consistently they follow only Chinese traditional conventions, applicable to Chinese painting, to be used by Chinese art students. Why each Canon should consist of two separate parts is not quite clear, unless it be to stress with equal importance the Content and the Art Form of a work of art.

CANON I. CH'I-YUN, SHENG-TUNG. Pertains to Spirit and the operation of Rhythmic Vitality that flows through all forms of nature.

CH'I-YUN. This relates to the aura or the rhythm of nature and is regarded as the most essential factor in a work of art. Its import seems undefinable, since it makes its appeal rather to the spirit of the observer than to his intellectual faculty. Some writers imply that its expression is a spontaneous outflow of the painter's own spirit.

Verifying this, Li-Po, the great poet and critic of the Sung dynasty, wrote: "The masterly paintings of ancient times were done by high-souled personages, men who renounced the world with its fame and riches, living virtuous lives in retirement, selecting art as one of the mediums for the expression of their noble sentiments."

That the high-minded soul or low character of the painter manifests itself unerringly through his calligraphy, painting or poetry is not to be questioned. However, not until he is made cognizant of the content as well as the art form expressed in the classic masterpieces—through the practice of copying them as prescribed in Canon VI—will his own spiritual qualities assert themselves and urge expression.

If the character of the artist is high and noble, and his urge forces the expression of his spiritual ideas, his production will be instinct with *Ch'i-yun* so that when he surveys an object of great beauty, at a given instant, he suddenly harnesses his own spirit to that of the great cosmic rhythm, which sets the currents of life in motion.

SHENG-TUNG. This consistently follows *Ch'i-yun,* and pertains to the operation of the movement of rhythmic vitality, which is thought to flow through all forms of nature.

In the consideration of this Canon, it must be apparent to the thoughtful analyst that the great masterpieces of art not only must be expressive of the spirituality of the painter, but also of his profound training.

(80)

And again, the discernment of Ch'i-yun Sheng-tung in a painting is dependent likewise upon both the esthetic and moral qualities of the beholder. Neither the materially-minded, worldly individual, nor the unsophisticated, who has never contacted the philosophies of the great religions, nor had the opportunity of acquiring the fundamentals of great art, nor of seeing the great masterpieces, can possibly have attained the esthetic sense necessary to comprehend the qualities of great art.

CANON II. KU-FA YUNG-PI. Pertains to form—objective. Anatomical structure. Brush and ink technique; wet lines.

KU-FA. This relates to the recognition of the structure of natural things, as well as to their laws of growth. As all principles of art are sound by virtue of their having been derived from nature, this structure should be seriously observed in the portrayal of any object, either animate or inanimate.

If a painting ignores the former, it is said to be boneless; if it fails to regard the latter, it is said to be inorganic. For example in the portrayal of a tree, the relative sizes of the trunk, boughs, branches and twigs, as well as the increased size of the feature at the point of outgrowth, must be considered.

YUNG-PI. This expands the processes of calligraphy, since painting is the outgrowth of calligraphy.

It describes the particular conditions under which the student may work to advantage, regulating the correct posture of the body, including the proper handling of the arm, at shoulder, elbow, wrist and fingers; the holding of the brush erect with the entire hand and arm unsupported —all of which combine to facilitate a free, unhampered and continuous movement.

"Dots and dashes" are habitually used for accentuation, as well as for giving the last touches to a painting to provide the necessary clarity and legibility.

For all the strokes referred to in this Canon, the student is directed to work with a brush well charged with ink, producing a solid black line, familiarly known as the "wet line," which has a more or less hard and tight quality consistent with a factual and scientific rendition required for a literal portrayal.

These conditions provide for a series of exercises consisting of intensive drills on the practice of lines—singly or in combination—which must be executed with one controlled movement of the brush, never resorting to repairs. The lines practiced should be either fine or coarse, or graduating from fine to coarse or the reverse; the brush must ever be dexterously manipulated, with various degrees of pressure, generally beginning and ending with the so-called "nail-heads."

These exercises also include practice on "dots and dashes," a form of short strokes which disregard the "nail-heads" previously described, and continue with an ever-widening stroke from beginning to end, as found in the drawing of a bamboo leaf.

CANON III. YING-WU HSIANG-HSING. Pertains to form—subjective. Abstractions organically conceived. The expansion of brush and ink technique from wet lines to dry lines.

YING-WU. This relates to Abstractions. The earliest examples of pictorial representation never were exact imitations of nature, but simple renditions of the barest essentials necessary to convey the content. The thought regarding this is well expressed in the poem by Su Tung-p'o, of the Sung dynasty, in which he says: "He who values a picture for its resemblance to nature has a cultural faculty near to that of a child." This theory is likewise held by a Western author who maintains: "Creative art begins where nature ends."

In China all Abstractions consist of brief portrayals of poetic significance—the very acme of the refinement known as fenglui. These, produced by the elimination of all non-essentials, were ever mindful of the fundamentals governing the structural forms of nature, and never descended to deformation, distortion, or misplacement of essential features, except in cases where

(82)

extreme caricature was intended. Abstractions, common to the contemporary art of the West, which ignore the organisms of the forms of nature, had no parallel in the art of the Orient.

From time immemorial, the Chinese have created Abstractions of great beauty, particularly of animal forms—both real and fabulous. A notable example is the familiar dragon, a composite creature of pure invention, which borrowed its members from a number of different animals, but still adhered to the structural organism of all quadrupeds.

One of the most remarkable and beautiful examples of ancient Abstractions may still be seen in the Great Tomb of Gukenri, in Korea, dating from 565 A.D. This consists of a colored mural of four paintings, representing the animal guardians of the four directions—the Dragon, the Phoenix, the Tiger, and the Dark Warrior—the Tortoise entwined by the Serpent. Each is consistently rendered in an abstract art form of great beauty, yet following the structure of its progenitor.

Another instance of Abstractions which occurs on wall decoration, may be found in the sepulchral bas-reliefs of the Wu Shrines in the province of Shantung. These were done during the Han dynasty; second century B.C. to second century A.D., and include Abstractions ranging from the human form to that of every kind of animal life, as well as background accessories, including trees of beautiful pattern.

Other sources of Abstractions may be found on bronzes of great antiquity, among which are mythological animals and birds. Together with floral scrolls of foliated rectangular spirals suggesting clouds and mist, they form a background to the visage of the ogre known as *t'ao-tieh*. In the usual portrayals of animals, such features as the plumage of birds and the scales of fish are abstract in the sense that they are conventionalized or stylized into regular arrangements of carefully drawn patterns.

The arts of all peoples began with Abstractions. From the ancient civilizations of both Central and South America many such have survived, some of which have characteristics resembling the Abstractions of the Far East. One instance may be seen in the Peruvian fish pattern, which structurally is like the *Tai Che* or the *aa-Kwa* of the Chinese.

All iconography of the various Oriental religions is markedly abstract. The Mohammedans, in particular, who regarded all portraiture of natural forms as a type of idolatry, produced abstract art of great beauty, consisting of arabesques, rosettes, and motives based largely on geometric forms. Again Celtic art, with its interlacing bands of geometric forms, also offers many Abstractions of rare charm.

Another principle involved in abstract art is that of paucity. This prescribes that not only shall there be sparseness in the number of features used to convey the idea of the subject, but also in the number of parts which constitute each, since redundancy is ever regarded as the very antithesis of a fine art.

HSIANG-HSING. This calls for an expansion of the brush and ink technique required for the production of "wet lines," into the processes necessary for "dry lines," as well as for those necessary for washes.

The method for "dry lines" directs that the brush, with hairs spread—charged sparingly with ink and little moisture—shall be freely used with speed, freedom and spontaneity. Then, when wielded by a technician of power, it will produce a stroke having parts of untouched ground, with edges ragged and uneven, picturesque as well as esthetic in quality—a stroke which should reflect the character of the painter.

It is said of Wu Tao-Tzu, of the T'ang dynasty—who was not only one of the greatest painters of Oriental art and Occidental as well—that so great was his ability that he actually breathed life into his very brush strokes. He is credited with having painted the aureole of a divinity with one sweep, manifesting such power that it seemed as if his brush were directed by a whirlwind in the hand of a god.

(84)

The brush and ink technique required for the painting of washes calls for drills through a sequence of exercises ranging from the production of flat tones of uniform values of light or dark to those which graduate from light to dark, or the reverse. For all washes, the processes are fundamentally the same: i.e. the brush stroke begins on the left at the top of the area to be covered, and moves horizontally to the right, each succeeding stroke carrying along the surplus fluid of the former stroke, until the surface has been completely covered. Then the pools that collect in the lower part are taken up by a dry fan-shaped brush.

The difference, between the process of painting a uniform wash and one that is graduated, lies in that for the former the ink is the same for each stroke, whereas, for a graduated wash, that is to range from dark to light, the brush is fully charged with ink for the first stroke, and for each successive stroke it is dipped into clear water, so that each stroke becomes lighter, until the original ink intensity is lost.

When the wash is to graduate from light to dark, the brush is charged with clear water, then gradually ink is added, until the original water has been exhausted and the fluid of the brush is of the full intensity of the ink.

Many drills are required to accomplish the desired result, since it not only calls for great skill in wielding the brush, but also for the exercise of a keen judgment pertaining to the required quantity of either water or ink. Different forms of washes are an important factor in a painting, and demand a most skillful brush virtuosity, for which many exercises of intensive drills are required.

CANON IV. SUI-LEI FU-TS'AI. Pertains to color. Oriental and Occidental color compared. Methods of producing pigments and dyes. Color, emblematic and symbolic.

SUI-LEI. This relates to the particular hue or chroma of a pigment or dye, that corresponds to the particular hue or chroma sensed by the physical eye.

The outstanding characteristic of Chinese painting is its exceptionally beautiful color quality, a quality distinguished for its soft radiant warmth, subordination, and spirituality which engenders a psychological reaction of calmness and tranquillity.

This characteristic is quite in contrast with its counterpart of the western world, where normal standards, derived from scientific sources, are cold, hard, lifeless, vividly intense, capable of causing a mental reaction of disturbance and restlessness.

So marked is the difference between the two schools that sophisticated critics habitually, in the esthetic attribution of a work of art, will refer to its color as being either Oriental or Occidental.

That the particular quality of Chinese color fails to imitate objectively the colors sensed by the physical eye is entirely due to conditions, the principal one of which was the complicated native processes of producing the dyes and pigments.

This is particularly true of the dyes. One of these processes is described as digging holes in the beds of streams, where all sorts of refuse, particularly vegetable, collected. This was then ground together indiscriminately into a substance from which dyes of varying hues were obtained.

The results of such a procedure could not fail to be accidental, hence incapable of being repeated in order to match any color in mind.

They likewise were not only variable, but fugitive, which unquestionably was the cause for quite a few existing "misfits" in painting.

In addition to the above, dyes were derived exclusively from vegetable juices: yellow, from the sap of rattan; blue, from indigo; black, from Chinese inks made from the soot of plants mixed with oil.

Other colors were obtained entirely from minerals: green, from malachite and jade; blue, from lapis lazuli; red, from cinnabar, and coral; yellow, from orpiment; and white, from white lead or burnt oyster shells; gold and silver, from the actual metal, used in either leaf or powder form, and the dyes were frequently mineralized by adding Chinese white ink.

Another factor contributing to the rare quality of the color of Chinese painting consists in the native feeling for harmonious combinations, as well as for the juxtaposition of colors which have the power of vivifying each other, suggestive of an understanding of complementaries used by designers of the West. The Chinese also manifest a knowledge of the variability of light, dark and intensity effects due to the size of the area covered.

The Chinese from remote times indulged in color Abstractions, mainly monochromatic by which the paintings consisted of the self-tones of a single color, principally black. For they claimed that in the lustrous quality of the best black inks the hues of all colors could be discerned.

However, the monochromatic Abstraction was not always black. The poet, Su Tung-p'o painted his bamboos red, and when asked: "Why red, when there are no red bamboos?" He replied: "Why black, when there is no such thing as black bamboo?"

An example of similar import is given pertaining to an American designer who made the deer of his composition green, and when asked why, replied: "In certain realms of the imagination, deer are green."

Quite true! Art ideas proceed from the realm of the imagination, in consequence of which they are licensed to manifest themselves in terms of parables and symbols, through highly evolved conventions, which frequently are quite enigmatical.

The earliest Chinese painting was done on silk, but with the invention of paper the silk was kept for copy work, while the artist's original compositions were done on paper. In a Western sense Chinese painting is known as water color; oil painting, as such, being unknown.

Erudition in this exotic art is rare, even in its own domain. Literature on the subject is

(87)

sparse and not always illuminating. Anyway, art must be seen to be known, appreciated and enjoyed. For the latter purpose, the student is obliged to have recourse to museums and private collections. But, unfortunately, the examples shown are apt to be misleading, since they mainly have been collected for their archeological, historical or purely technical worth; their esthetic value being determined from the standpoint of, "what was," instead of "what is." For, that their original beauty has vanished—due to the inroads of devastating activities of centuries, when light, heat and humidity wrought unhappy changes in dyes and pigments—seems to have been disregarded, notwithstanding the confusing illegible product of "what is."

The reverence for the old made the paintings of antiquity set the standards of values. However, there were some who realized the folly of such a belief. Wang Ch'i-chang of the sixteenth century was one such. He is quoted as having written: "A picture will be at its best for only five hundred years. After that, it deteriorates. After eight hundred years, its spirit has fled; and after it has reached a thousand years, there absolutely is nothing left."

It is to be regretted—inasmuch as there are still available examples of Chinese painting of great beauty, paintings which not only may inspire the serious student, but stimulate his imagination toward subject matter while revealing new methods of technique—that museums should waste valuable wall space to display a work that is so far gone, it is difficult to know whether it is right side up, or upside down.

FU-TS'AI. This signifies "to apply color," and has a dual function. One relates to processes of technique which prescribe the progression from the brush and ink exercises to drills in the use of water colors; the other, to its application to things emblematic and symbolic.

The technical drills prescribe exercises using single colors for washes of flat uniform value; of graduated values; and of several colors graduating into each other, ultimately culminating in painting scales of the solar spectrum. Then exercises in color mixing and color matching should follow.

The first may be regarded as purely an experimental venture, designed to inculcate familiarity

(88)

with the chemistry of pigments, as well as with the various color subtleties so that the component parts of a color, submitted for matching, may be discerned.

For the color mixing, any box of water colors, or even chalks, may be used. The water-color mixing may be done in a small receptacle or on paper, where one color may be painted upon another. The same may be done for mixing the chalks.

For the color matching, oriental textiles may be of value. These should be colorful, yet having the quality of *feng-liu*, which is the very epitome of refinement.

The second significance of "to apply color" relates to its special usages for things, themselves emblematic or symbolic. It is said that originally the Chinese had but five colors: black, white, red, blue and yellow. These were used arbitrarily as emblems and symbols for particular things. For example, in the portrayal of the Gods of the Four Directions, the Dragon of the East is shown blue; the Crow of the South, red; the Tiger of the West, white; the Dark Warrior of the North, black; all four surrounding a central pivotal point, yellow.

Correspondingly, blue became the symbol of Spring, life and happiness; white of Autumn, peace and tranquillity; red, of Summer, festivities and pleasure; black of Winter, sorrow and death.

Again, the ever present Imperial yellow is consciously symbolic of the Emperor, while white ever suggests mourning, and a soft radiant blue commonly recalls the spiral ringlets of the Lama Pu-sa.

CANON V. CHING-YING WEI-CH'I. Pertains to composition. Consideration of organism and pattern movements; lines; spots; spaces, and values. Combinations of related things.

CHING-YING. This relates to the composition of a picture and prescribes the rules which dominate its structure or organism—rules which likewise apply to the arrangements of three-dimensional objects.

For Canon V as for Canon III, Simplicity is a fundamental requirement. Likewise the law of Relativity must be observed; for only through harmonious relationships of the component parts of a composition, can the organism perform its chief function of expressing Unity.

To envision an Organism, such as would be required for a picture of Bamboo, the latter's actual features—the stalks, stems, nodes, and leaves—should be transposed into technical terms of art diction, such as Lines, Spots, Spaces and Values.

In the consideration of "Lines," the word line is apt to cause confusion, since it is variously used to express different ideas. Ordinarily, it means a brush stroke drawn between two opposite points, but in the usage here applied, it signifies "direction," as in speaking of the line of a garment.

In a pictorial composition, like that which may be required for a subject such as Bamboo, "Lines" refer to the "directional movements" of the stalks and stems, which determine the structure or anatomy of the organism. There are two kinds of the latter in every picture—the actual and the occult.

The actual Lines are self-evident, while the occult, frequently referred to as the "line of attraction," are purely imaginative, consisting of the observer's "eye-passage," impelled psychologically by special interest through the main features or spots of the composition, and having no relationship with the fundamental structure.

To clarify the significance of organism, the skeletalization of several pictures may prove helpful. This may be done by making a lead pencil tracing on transparent paper of the actual "directional" lines of each painting, revealing varying results. In some there will be a frank admission of adherence to established art principles, while in others there will be a serious violation of them.

Tracings made from the best Chinese paintings show a group of "directional" lines converging toward a single source of growth, placed imaginatively beyond the enclosing rectangle. Such lines do not diverge nor cross each other—for divergence and crossed lines stimulate the psychological reaction of diversity and discord, instead of unity and harmony.

The skeletalization above referred to, in addition to revealing the structural lines of the composition, likewise divide the entire field of the composition into two equivalent areas, providing spaces—one for the "pattern" of the picture, and the other for the "no pattern" or vacancy, quite in accordance with the significance and function of the Chinese Great Monad, the *Yang* and *Yin*.

The latter classifies all things under two great categories of balancing contrasting opposites, such as the masculine and feminine; light and darkness; good and evil; action and rest. This is quite adaptable to two dimensional art, by using the *Yang* for the "pattern," and the *Yin* for the "no pattern," or vacant space.

The vacant space sometimes is referred to as "The space of silence," and again as "The emptiness of the void," the significance of which was so ardently sought by the Taoists, and of which Lao-tzu, the great philosopher, said, "has its counterpart in the hollow of a clay vessel, which alone makes it serviceable." The balance above referred to is not one of absolute symmetry, but one in which the artistic license of variation is permissible.

Continuing the consideration of the remaining compositional features, spots and their associate spaces require attention. A spot, in a composition portraying Bamboo, may consist of a single feature, such as a Bamboo leaf, a cluster of leaves, or a group of clusters, and for the arrangement of which the principle of Irregularity should prevail, which quite consistently prohibits their being placed in a continuous line horizontally, vertically, obliquely, or at equal intervals.

A specific principle—which the writer has found of value in teaching and designing—has been designated as the "Two together and One Apart" principle, which is quite in accord with the well known and much used law of Principality and Subordination, of Occidental origin.

Regarding spaces; these may be large or small; the large ones resulting from the *Yang* and

Yin divisions of the area, while the small ones are those which naturally fall between the spots. Designers generally regard the shapes of spaces almost as seriously as the shapes of spots.

Should the arrangement of spots violate the given principles, there follows what sophisticated designers call "spottiness"; and, in their estimation, "spottiness" is the worst criticism to be made of a piece of two-dimensional art.

Frequently, and quite erroneously, "spottiness" is regarded as a form of Rhythm, particularly when the latter is confused with Repetition, which consists of mere pulsations recurring from static and fixed periods like the ticks of time and heartbeats.

Rhythm on the other hand is quite different, it being temporal and mobile. Its pulsations vary in length and movements, generally following simple, flowing, streamlined curves of different elevations.

Values is another and most important factor of a composition. It applies to both pictorial and decorative art. It is by virtue of a distinguishing contrast of either color or tone, that a spot is outstanding in contrast to its surroundings.

The Values of the spots and spaces must be such as to produce a separateness, to clarify the definition of the pattern; and then by transition of intensities, ranging from the strong to the weak, either advance or recede, and thereby express nearness and distance, as well as effects of atmosphere and aerial perspective.

Should the important Values of a composition be misplaced with regard to planes of distance—such as the foreground, mid-distance and background—there occurs what is known as a "Reversal of Values," causing an unhappy confusion in the picture.

Values is generally the weak point in all art, Oriental as well as Occidental. This is particularly noticeable in outline portrayal by the Chinese. It is not uncommon to see a full length

(92)

portrait, particularly in stone rubbings, where the face and hand features are practically lost, while the figures' apparel carries strongly across a room, due to the Chinese custom of using fine brushes exclusively for what are regarded as important features, and coarse brushes for the figures' clothing. The same is true in floral compositions, where the blossoms sink into insignificance in contrast with the foliage.

WEI-CH'I. This prescribes rules to govern the selection of objects to be combined in a picture. The subjects painted by the Chinese include everything to be found in the Three Kingdoms; and the training of the art student has prepared him, not only to portray all these things ranging from rocks to man himself, but to select for his composition things that are related by the content of their subject matter.

For example, the combination poetically known as *Ssu Chun-tzu*, "The Four Gentlemen," consists of the plum, orchid, chrysanthemum and Bamboo. They were chosen because they symbolize the ideal of gentlemanly behavior, who were quite frequently referred to as "That Sir!"— the Bamboo in particular being designated as the "long-body gentleman." They likewise symbolized "longevity," not however a longevity of lingering decadence, but one of perennial rejuvenation.

Another popular combination is that of the "Bamboo and Tiger." It is held that when the tiger is pursued by the elephant, he takes refuge in a Bamboo grove, whither the elephant cannot follow on account of his size. Therefore, the Bamboo has acquired the additional symbolism of refuge or security.

Again a popular combination is that of the "Bamboo and Sparrow." This is due to the habit of the gentle little songster, voicing its injunction, *chu, chu, chu,* "be loyal," "be loyal," "be loyal," from slender Bamboo stalks. It therefore follows consistently that the two could be combined in the graphic arts.

CANON VI. CHUAN-MO I-HSIEH. Pertains to the perpetuity of ancient ideals. Studying masterpieces of all times, and transmitting the principles governing them,
as to subject matter, as well as to technique.

CHUAN-MO. This relates to the study of classic models in order that the student may acquire standard ideals—a practice which has continued from the most ancient days down to the present time, extending over a period of four thousand years.

But in order that the student may be sure of the truth of these ideals, before he appropriates them in his own work, he should, as St. Paul in his message to the Thessalonians admonished, "Prove all things and hold fast to that which is good." But in advance of this he likewise should have been given a clear conception regarding the true function of art.

For the latter, St. Paul may again be helpful in solving a question discussed through the ages, when he says: "Whatsoever things are true; whatsoever things are honorable; whatsoever things are just; whatsoever things are pure; whatsoever things are lovely; whatsoever things are of good report; if there be any virtue, and if there be any praise, think on these things." Does not this relate to "the good, the true, and the beautiful"?

The Chinese have ever held that art should be closely related to life, ever administering to the uplift of human character, never lending itself in any way to ignoble thought or action. Then, if this be true, would it not be the chief function of Art to express Beauty—a beauty that may soothe and pacify this disturbing human sense of things? For is not harmony, or its pursuit, actually the goal of man? And is not beauty the language of harmony? Then should not Art be the vehicle for the expression of Beauty?

But in addition to the acquisition of the ideals, as well as a knowledge of the function of Art, the Chinese student should likewise be impressed with the virtue of training—a training involving years in which he concentrates his life to Art and submits to the most intensive instruction and laborious drills, directed to the perfection of technique; a training which involves drills on processes of tracing, reducing, enlarging and copying—first simple compositions, then the masterpieces.

(94)

After that, he is ready to attach himself to a master, and with him is able to venture happily into the field of observation. This stimulates thought and induces invention. He becomes creative. He has attained his freedom even from the thought of technique and works with an unhampered spontaneity quite worthy of the reputation of being an artist—something infinitely greater than a painter, who at best may be only a craftsman.

Surely the Chinese wisely understood the value of fundamental preparation. His simple compositions and epigrammatic renditions of beauty were no accidents, but carefully planned and wrought results. It is a common saying with the Chinese that the preparation of an artist is of such consequence that, before he can regard himself as worthy to paint a real picture, "he must read ten thousand books, travel ten thousand miles, and have a grounding in general culture, or his brush will betray the erring wilfullness of a child who thinks he can run before he can walk, or practice geometry without the aid of Pythagoras."

While unquestionably such training led to the efflorescence of Chinese painting, it also, when misunderstood and misapplied by many who followed the mere letter, resulted in a serious continued decadence of the art, until it now fails to even echo the spirit of the past.

I-HSIEH. This relates to the copying of ancient masterpieces, a practice which began with Hsieh Ho and has since persisted.

Chinese literature abounds with references to the esteem in which the ancient works were held, and to the value of copying them. That this copying was no mere mechanical imitation of the art form and the personal style and conventions of the painter is proved in many statements of famous critics. One writes: "True copying consists in transferring the thought rather than the exact lines of a picture." Another repeats: "While it is not difficult to reproduce the art form, to transfer the spirit of the artist is quite another matter."

Such copying was not limited to the work of the ancient masters exclusively, but included that of various dynasties, so that the student might appropriate for his own work the chief characteristics of different periods.

(95)

An illustration of the latter is related to Tung-Ch'ang, one of the foremost artists of the Ming dynasty, who, in addition to fulfilling his duties as President of the Board of Public Rites, also followed the profession of painting. "He so loved this art that he spent his leisure copying the masters, with such zeal that he forgot to eat and sleep."

Regarding his own painting, he said: "In my youth, I studied Huang Kung-wang for landscape, but in middle life I turned to the models of the Sung dynasty. Then comparing my work with that of Weng T'ung, I found that each of us had his own individual merits and defects. His perfection of form and brush work, I could not hope to rival, though in refinement and finish I was in advance of him."

As to the successful application of the rules of these Six Canons, the inventor himself has said: "It ever has been rare for anyone to qualify in all. One exception was that of Lu Tan-wei; he was marvelous not only in conception, but in execution as well, becoming a model for modern painters as well as those of his own generation."

In the subject matter of his own work, where the things portrayed ranged from the mineral through the vegetable and animal kingdoms, he ever revealed their inherent characteristics—such as the fierceness of the tiger, the strength of the lion, the swiftness of the horse, and the soul of the flower.

But, again, that the real artist was no mere copyist of other men's works may be inferred from the following admonition of the famous artist and scribe of the Sung dynasty, Kuo Hsi, who says:

Cultivate a full and artistic spirit;
Observe vividly and comprehensively;
Acquire a varied and extensive experience;
Take in the essentials of the scene,
and discard trivialities.

In addition, however, to the knowledge and power acquired through adherence to the principles given in the Canons, the modern student—in order to come to a full realization of what was entailed in the educational preparation for efficiency—should become imbued with the following admonitions:

He must have his mind filled with the historical and
  traditional legends of his country;
He must know the principles of the philosophy of life
  and the symbols which represent them;
He must become familiar with the Classics and have his heart
  moved by the great achievements of the past;
He must fill his soul with spiritual culture while training
  his hand to manual dexterity; and
He must preserve unchanged the same art spirit even though
  the earthly examples perish.

But, above and beyond all, agreeing with Cicero, he must learn that the true Function of Art is fundamentally to train the mind to high thinking, and the heart to worthy sentiments.

THE PSYCHOLOGY OF GRAPHIC ART

Insofar as art is so commonly regarded as a matter of psychology, and that this subject is so frequently referred to through the pages of this volume, particularly in the elucidation of the "Canons of Hsieh Ho," it seems of the greatest importance that it be clearly defined.

A survey of the arts of all peoples, in all times and under all conditions, reveals that, while graphic expression is ever in a state of flux, progressing and retrogressing and progressing again, its fundamental impulses are psychologically directed. Hence the mental reactions, Oriental and Occidental alike, become the determining factors of the esthetic worth of art production.

However, the character and quality of these mental operations are dependent upon the educational status of the individuals who constitute the examining jury. Therefore the greatest care should be exercised in the selection of this group, before accepting verdicts pertaining to judgments of art principles and standards of excellence.

Since psychology is such a common word and pertains to so many activities—benefic and malefic—it is quite necessary to understand that the particular kind here referred to is that which is related to the graphic arts, and pertains to the mental stimuli induced by pictures.

For example, the emotions of uplift and exaltation felt in a forest interior—generally attributed to some indefinable mysterious influence of nature—is in reality caused by the upward, perpendicular directional line tendency of the towering trees. Similarly, the sense of calm and tranquillity, as well as of monotony and depression, felt while gazing at a level plain or prairie, may be attributed to the dominating horizontal directional line tendency of these features. While again the sense of insecurity and disturbance induced by the slanting lines of leaning trees or telegraph poles, or the zigzag lines or lightning flashes across the sky, may likewise be attributed to like directional line tendencies.

In each case, the cause is mainly sensorious due to the mental stimulation of the sense of sight.

A mental experiment may be of value in clarifying these postulates. For example, imagine the walls of three adjoining rooms decorated with parallel straight lines—one with all vertical, another with all horizontal, and the third with all oblique—and note the psychological difference in each: that of the vertical line pattern should be inspiring and uplifting; that of the horizontal, gloomy and depressing; while that of the oblique will not only be confusing, but be as unsettling as the rocking of a ship in a storm.

From experiments with straight lines, others may proceed similarly with curved lines. Of this group the spiral has the most to offer psychologically. As a single line—proceeding from a center with the potentiality of continuing indefinitely—its open end portends infinite existence with perpetual progression. Its shape is quite common in nature. In the plant world it appears in the tendrils of vines; and again in the boundary edges of sea-shells, where, however, its terminal closes in on itself.

Planes and solids, likewise have psychological reactions. The square and cube, as well as the circle and sphere, have distinctly different appeals. The cube is static and never disturbs. In other words, "it stays put," while the sphere is mobile and prone to locomotion, rolling unhappily until interrupted by an obstacle. On the other hand, the soothing characteristics of its uninterrupted single smooth face of uniform convexity presents an appeal quite gratifying. The cube, however, notwithstanding its six plane unobtrusive faces has, not only eight sharp edges, but eight sharp pointed corners, which are apt to be rasping. So strongly has this been felt that the esthetically conscious craftsman has rounded off these offending members from most of his rectangular objects. Again, these two solids, the cube and sphere, have another kind of appeal, pleasing in one category and quite the reverse in another. For example: the cube being static, its incapacity to move suggests the instinctive, stationary sense of "Balance" which man has developed through the eons, in his perpetual efforts to maintain the erect position required for that greatest of all miracles—walking. The sphere, however, in contrast to the cube, being mobile, stimulates the sense of Rhythm. While the sense of Balance is inherent fundamentally, and spontaneously natural, the sense of Rhythm is pure acquisition and evolution. Hence Balance and Rhythm may be regarded as another example of the contrast of opposites, comparable to the *tai-chi* or *yang and yin* of the Taoists.

Balance is fixed, static; Rhythm is unfixed and mobile. Balance represents inertia, inactivity and an uncompromising mental attitude and intolerance; while Rhythm, quite the reverse represents movement and pulsation, reacting in a sense of ever-flowing, and an attitude of yielding. Rhythm is one of the most important factors in art. It not only makes a strong appeal to the imagination, but has the power to still disturbed emotions, "leaving a calmness, in the instinctive empathic sense, that reacts in an expression of delight."

Since the cube and the sphere are the basis of so large a class of familiar objects of usage, it has been felt important to treat the psychology of these two solids very definitely, in order that the student may apply the principles involved, while making the appraisement of their esthetic worth.

Again, in addition to a separate psychology stimulated by the geometric form of solids, there is likewise a psychology proceeding from ordinary things relating to their surface characteristics Color and Texture.

Color in particular has a strong psychological appeal, and wherever seen in graphic or textile portrayal, should stimulate reactions of charm, exhilaration and joy; that is, provided it is actually color, and reveals the particular quality which the esthetic erudite regards as *feng-liu*, the very epitome of refinement, as stated in Canon IV.

Quite frequently, in common parlance, words relating to this subject are used, which, unfortunately, are misleading to the art untutored. "Color," should express unity, manifesting a harmonious relationship whatever the intensity of the hue, or tempo of the key of values. Again, "a composition of colors," and "a color composition," have separate meanings. The former being polychromatic or a mosaic of varying qualities of hue, can accidentally result in a harmonious relationship, but it is more likely to consist of hues: vivid, crude, cold and hard, which, consciously or unconsciously, irritate the observer into unhappy emotions. The word "coloring" may mean anything, and there is no such word as the much used "colorings." According to the esthetic status of an observer, color or colors may delight or repulse him; excite or depress him; and they likewise have been credited with the power to exercise black magic. The Chinese cite an instance where mental murder was committed by the incarceration of the victim in a room colored exclusively with a "violent red."

Texture likewise has its special appeal. Teachers of design include in their exercises on this subject problems of pattern, in which they utilize bits of paper, silk, cotton, wool, hemp, metal and rocks; some have surfaces rough or smooth, dull or shiny, or mirroring; each having its own psychological reaction.

The individual with well-developed esthetic sense will respond to the subtlety of the crystal, due to its reflective powers, while being repelled or offended by the tinsel and glitter of highly polished surfaces. When this reflective power is enhanced by color and motion, as in the soap-bubble, there is a distinctly natural mobile of great beauty and charm.

This aspect of motion—long used by the Chinese in their wind-catching devices—is now being used by craftsmen of the West in most attractive color *Abstractions*. These mobiles of recent production offer a wide scope for invention and the play of the creative imagination.

In the observance of the exceptional manifestations of pattern of great interest and beauty resulting from the changing forms of the cosmic element of water—such as steam, mist, fog, clouds, rain and snow—the human mind may experience psychological reactions, and a variety of emotions, both happy and unhappy.

Reflections—whether occurring in still scenes on placid waters of streams, or dancing merrily on wet pavements during a gentle rain—are ever alluring. Shadows are always poetically suggestive, especially so of tree foliage cast on asphalt roads. Then, when there is a combination of both Reflections and Shadows, as described in the poem, "*The white walls tremble in the shadowy waves,"* there is a dual attraction. The Javanese early were cognizant of the beauty of shadows, to which their Shadow Dramas still testify.

Also smoke—which is so apt to suggest destruction—may stimulate an esthetic reaction when its uncoiling volumes of spiral shapes are seen from afar vanishing into the ether. Then again, displays of fireworks—in which forceful, luminous lines radiate from the source of explosion, and burst into a semblance of multicolored stars—likewise, thrill the observer.

But it is against the great sky-dome that the panorama is perpetually enacted. There the gentle clouds of mackerel and goose-feather types, pattern themselves so tenderly against the "blue"; or the dark forbidding storm-warners, threaten disaster; while lofty pink and white cumuli and their variants—native of southern seas—formed in perpendicular columns, sail in all their majesty just above the horizon, a veritable "Procession of the Heavenly Hosts."

There also is a particular psychology which dominates human behavior, the effects of which are dependent upon the status of two determining factors. The first consists of the intellectual and spiritual levels of the individual, manifested by a dominant ruling psyche—a psyche which has been evolved through eras of experience while in transit from "clod to God"—so ably expressed by Edwin Miller Wheelock in his remarkable treatise, "Proteus."

The second of these factors is a proficient education of the individual—an education covering the sublime heritage of the art of the past, a heritage of supreme works of art—that has been achieved and preserved through the centuries by people ranging from the savage to the sage.

The evolutionary status of spiritual and esthetic consciousness differs in every individual and manifests itself by questions commonly asked of a lecturer, becoming a reminder of the words of Aeschylus, in his powerful picture of man before he received the gift of divine fire from Prometheus:

For in the outset, eyes they had and saw not;
And ears they had, but heard not;
Age on age, like unsubstantial shapes in vision seen,
They groped at random in the world of sense.

It is likewise interesting to note that the Orientals of antiquity held similar views regarding the intellectual and spiritual status of mankind. To the Confucians is attributed the classification of the five fixed stations of existence designated as *Ch'u Hsin, Yi, Nung, M'iao* and *Chen,* which may be defined as follows: *Ch'u Hsin,* "The Awakening": The beginning of an awareness, or the recognition of *Feng-Liu,* that so markedly characterizes the greatest of Chinese art.

Yi, "The Idea": The consciousness of the thought involved; the significance; the path discovered.

Nung, "The can do": The discovery of ability.

M'iao, "The Marvel of It": The accomplishment beyond expectation. Talent manifested; attempts at invention; perfection of technique.

Che'n, "The Divine Power" or "God-given Genius"—of which there is but one example in a century, whereas of the fourth, there are as many as stars in the sky.

Since each life is supposed to be a fixed station, its understanding and expression must be limited; and regarding its potentiality for growth, the great philosophers have made no comment.

With this theory in mind, it will not be difficult to account for the great variety of ideas that exist regarding beauty and art, or for the ever-recurring question, "Is it Art?—the Art that will bring to this generation a 'spiritual freedom,' which will be 'As the leaves to the tree, for the healing of the nations.' "

ANALYSIS OF THE ILLUSTRATIONS

The examples herewith shown belong to what the Chinese call the "Literary Man's Painting," a style which for centuries has dominated the work of artists, as well as that of the popular taste.

The absence of color is not regarded as a lack, since black is felt to include all color,—as stated on page 87, of Canon IV.

The special art of calligraphy had, in ancient times, reached such a superlative degree of virtuosity that it is said of the writings of Wang Hsi—321-329, A.D. that his script was as light as the floating clouds and as vigorous as a startled dragon.

The relationship of calligraphy to painting is most evident in the earliest brushings of Bamboo, where the ideograph representing the word for this giant grass is shown transformed into its semblance. And while the serious portrayal began with mere attenuations of the tangible, it proceeded through various modifications, gradually and continuously becoming more and more factual, until it merged into an approximation of the pictorial.

In the consideration of these illustrations, it should be borne in mind that, while they are only reproductions, they reflect the atmosphere, beauty and artistry of the originals. However, no analysis of any picture can be final and illuminating, unless the student has been schooled in the laws which govern its Content as well as its Art Form.

Of the Content much information has been given on preceding pages, while the Art Form has been quite definitely treated on pages 89 through 93 of Canon V, and pages 81 and 82 of Canon II and pages 82 through 85 of Canon III.

In reviewing the preceding pages of this volume, the reader will find references to many kinds of Bamboo. For example, on page 76, it is related that the painter Cheng T'ang of the Yuan dynasty visited the famous Mt. Omei, especially to see the Phoenix-tailed Bamboo, and there discovered the Bodhisat or P'u-sa variety.

Then later, he visited Elephant Hill in the same locality, where he found varieties known as the Purple, the Bitter, the Wind, the Tortoise Shell, and the Filial Piety.

And again on pages 25 and 26 of the "Translation of the Memorial" there are references to a small gnarled and twisted species that creeps along the ground, as well as to a plant whose leaves are as large as a sword-blade ten feet long.

It is interesting to note that this giant grass grows exclusively in clumps, forests and groves, but never in a single plant except under special nursery culture.

It is to be regretted that the particular variety depicted by our Imperial Prince Painter cannot be named. However, what is of greater import is the particular characterization of the foliage of the plant shown in every composition, a characterization marked by the posture and vitality of every leaf blade. For example, it is said that:

> *In fair weather, the leaves spread joyously;*
> *In rainy weather the leaves hang despondently;*
> *In windy weather the leaves cross each other confusedly;*
> *And in the early morning dew, they point up vigorously.*

There has been much speculation regarding the cause of this phenomenon. Could it be due to a dominating psyche, similar to the human psyche described on pages 99 through 104 of the chapter on "Psychology of the Graphic Arts"?

Again, the inscriptions on the pictures offer interesting matter, since they record the place where each painting was done or the condition under which the artist worked: as,

Painted after dinner on a cold winter's day.
Painted on the third day of the third month after a
summer shower.
Painted in a house called Pine-tree Moon.
Painted by candle-light after studying the Bamboo
during the daylight.

The love of nature has ever been instinctive with the Chinese. Painters were ever alert in observing the subtler aspects, as manifested in mist, fog and clouds, making effective background accessories to Bamboo subjects. They, however, are treated very subordinately, conforming to the principle of Yang and Yin, definitely given on pages 91 and 92 of Canon V.

Generally the two masses, the "pattern" and "no-pattern," or "space of silence," occupy practically equivalent areas, of irregular contours. This makes the pattern one-sided or asymmetrical, having a convex contour which should face the center of the open space. The latter is variously located in the composition—sometimes to the left, sometimes to the right, or toward one or another corner.

One of the greatest attractions of our pictures is the aerial perspective due to planes of distance represented by different degrees of value intensity. But the greatest factor of all is one of pure esthetics; a subtle something above and beyond all that the eyes see—something that must be felt, commonly acclaimed as "charm" which is quite akin to the "it" so popular in recent decades, when referring to the attractiveness of a great personality. This nameless quality exists in a work of graphic art, when it consists of an epigrammatic portrayal that has been done offhand with confidence, assurance, decision and despatch—becoming, as the Chinese say, a *su-lin*, "a little bit of something precious."

Again, a picture that has been done from memory, in the quietude of the studio after the painter has spent a long time—sometimes days—seriously imbibing all the characteristics of the subject by careful or serious study, during which time he has had revealed to him "the particular beauty that underlies all appearances."

Then finally, the analyst will be moved to question:

First, have these pictures a quality of largeness and spaciousness, that suggest Infinity?

Second, have they a tranquil nobility and a gentle restraint, yet a quivering vitality?

Third, do they inspire a desire for further study of this art?

Fourth, does the student ever return to them with a renewed delight?

Fifth, do they stimulate a sense of joyousness that becomes a perpetual solace to the soul?

Sixth, do they—through their universality of art expression—make a favorable appeal to all alike whether schooled or not in art erudition?

Seventh, do they urge the study of Laotze's "Tao," a study that may lure the student to proceed on "The Road in which the universe moves toward Righteousness"—a Righteousness, as defined in David Wilson's translation of the poem discovered in the Shu King, an ancient Chinese anthology, parts of which date back to the third millennium, B.C.

The Royal Road is Righteousness,
It's straight, without unevenness.
And private love and private hate,
It leaves aside by going straight;
On every side it gives a view
Forever clear, forever true;
And broad and easy 't is to know,
For him who has the heart to go.
The Royal Road shall never bend,
The Royal Road shall never end.

Thus endeth the pages of "*Bamboo, Its Cult and Culture*," that, if read and reread, will not only enable the student to assess the esthetic values of the given illustrations, but any work of graphic art.

The Divine Mind
is
Omnipotent, Omniscient, Omnipresent.

The Divine Eye penetrates all things
The Divine Ear hears all things inaudible.

A word though unimportant
May bring honor or shame.
Things fall from the top.
Chiang Yei.

Behold the king shall reign in
Righteousness
and the princes shall rule in judgment
and the work of
Righteousness
shall be
Peace
and the effects of
Righteousness
shall be quietness and assurance forever.
Isaiah.

www.ingramcontent.com/pod-product-compliance
Lightning Source LLC
Chambersburg PA
CBHW052037280526
45791CB00010B/2990